What Peopl

the HEROES blueprint

I was very impressed with Tim's message in The Heroes Blueprint. *His contrasting of "situational heroes" with "transformational heroes" really resonated with me. Tim's life and testimony are quite compelling. His writing is to-the-point and instructive. He understands men and the need for men to engage in deeper relationships and greater submission to a God who will be glorified through such commitment. Tim offers extremely practical ideas for better living-out our faith. You will not want to miss this opportunity. Read* The Heroes Blueprint, *and be forever changed!*

Dr. Bob Stouffer — Author of
Light or Darkness: Reclaiming The Light in Sports

"The Heroes Blueprint *is a tremendous tool which can be used by men who are coming along side other men in the mentoring/coaching process. Taking men through the 10 steps can give you great insight into what God has done in their lives and where he is taking them.*"

Al Lorenzen — CEO Wildwood Hills Ranch,
Former Professional Basketball Player

the HEROES blueprint

*10 Steps to Unleashing
Your Inner Hero*

TIM MITCHUM

HERO PUBLISHING LLC

the HEROES blueprint
10 Steps to Unleashing Your Inner Hero

TIM MITCHUM

ISBN 978-0-9822990-6-7 (paperback)
ISBN 978-0-9822990-7-4 (Epub)

Hero Publishing LLC
PO Box 765
Johnston, Iowa 50131
515-991-4740 Office

Cover and Interior Design by:
Bonnie Bushman
bbushman@bresnan.net

Printed in the United States of America

Dedicated to YOU, for taking the first step
to becoming the Transformational Hero
your loved ones deserve,
and the world desperately needs.
You will never be the same.

FOREWORD

Once I was past the flattery and honor of being asked to write the foreword to this book, I was faced with a blank page and the question: Now what? What do I write, where do I start? I know that if I were looking at buying a book like this, I would want to know a couple things: 1) Who is this author, Tim Mitchum? And, 2) Why the heck should I read this book? I think I can answer both those questions.

Who is Tim Mitchum?

I met Tim Mitchum a little over four years ago. He was a worship leader at the church my family and I attended. I was assigned to play guitar on his team for one Sunday each month. We immediately clicked, on stage and off. We shared similar interests, passions, and backgrounds. We both loved guitars and a well crafted song, no matter the genre. We had played and loved sports. Each of us had father wounds from emotionally or physically absent Dads. And, at one point of our lives, we stuck our toes in the waters of the "Wild Side," only to realize later that life is much more livable and lovable when striving to reach the fertile soils of righteousness. And we were both in the beginning stages of major life changes. My change was making the shift from an Information Technology Consultant to a full time Staff Songwriter for a music publisher in Nashville, Tennessee. It's a story in itself, but basically I was given the opportunity of a lifetime, and it meant a complete change in direction for my life, and my family's lives.

I thought my "Life-Change" was unconventional, but Tim's was one that I look back on with amazement. What was his change? He purposefully quit his job and completely wiped his life's plate clean of anything and everything! I've known many people, throughout my life, who say something like this, but never with the clarity or conviction that Tim had. Most people change jobs; some change careers; some may even move to a different town or city. They mostly make their life change because they've reached a pain threshold that can no longer be ignored, and they reach for what seems like the next best big move, only to realize that it's not the job or location that needed to change, but something within themselves.

Not so with Tim. At the time of this decision, he was experiencing a very successful sales and marketing career. He made a very comfortable living, and was happy doing what he was doing. Tim was living the American dream. He owned a nice house, had many friends, was a leader in his church, had the cool truck, car, and motorcycle. So, why was he not only quitting his job, but "wiping his plate clean?" Because "something bigger was calling him." He had no idea what it was or what it looked like. He just knew that he had leave his job, church and other involvements to give him the margin in his life to understand and get clarity around what "it" was. God was asking him to STOP EVERYTHING! He was being asked to "wait, listen and obey." Now we've all heard those little "soul whispers," but seriously, how many people do you know, directly or indirectly, who would be courageous enough to do this? I was in my early forties, and was about to witness this for the first time.

Over the next three years I saw, firsthand, what I call the dismantling and reassembly of Tim Mitchum. Now you may view that statement as a bit of a negative, but I look at it as the opposite. If I could draw a parallel, I would describe it as taking an already stylish and fast Corvette, stripping it down and tearing it apart, only to perform the upgrades that make it far more powerful, efficient, and appealing. It was the same with Tim, only neither of us had a clue at the time that the metaphoric "overhaul" and "evolution" would result in this book.

The dismantling phase, as I recall, was immediate and swift, although Tim would challenge the notion of swift, I'm sure. God seemed to rip off the hood and go to work. There were parts that needed tuning. There were parts that needed to be bored out or re-shaped, and there was a part or two that needed to be completely restored. Most, if not all, the men I know would have shied away from the vulnerability and pain it took to endure this process. But with every discovery of brokenness there was revelation, healing, growth, and new confidence. Not a swagger that comes from the human ego, but an inner confidence that comes from faith in something bigger than yourself.

I have to admit, I never truly understood the Scripture in *Corinthians 12:9*, referring to "God's power being made perfect in our weakness," but I saw its meaning unfold before my eyes.

Somewhere in the beginnings of the Tim Mitchum overhaul, he stumbled onto his most significant discovery, as he would tell you. He knew he wasn't measuring up, but didn't know what he was supposed to measure up to. He couldn't give definition to what it meant to be a man. He had no frame of reference on how be a man, let alone a Hero, nor did he understand when a man becomes a man. There was no blueprint that he could follow that he could base his smallest decisions on, nor his biggest desires. How could he measure himself as a man if he didn't have the tools and barometer to do so? How could he claim his manhood, if no one had ever shared with him what it was to be a man? Tim's biological father denied him his name, and did not acknowledge his existence for his entire life. Not only did he have no one to model manhood, but he also had wounds of rejection. He spent his life compensating, and guessing at life. (If you picked up this book, and are reading this far, I'm sure you can relate on some level.)

Some people may use this information as a crutch or an excuse, or claim themselves to be a victim, but not Tim. He owned it. He drove headlong into it. His already curious nature became honed in to anyone, anything, and everything that would give him more understanding, and a true definition of Manhood. He read books. He attended every seminar and group study he could. He sought out mentors. All the while, he was journaling his thoughts, progress, and findings. Over time, I noticed the worm starting to turn. HE was the one mentoring others. HE was the one leading various men's groups, volunteering his time to coach inner city kids, and speaking to various organizations, just to name a few. HE was the one armed with the answers. Tim Mitchum was now empowering others and forever changing lives; God's power made perfect in weakness.

I can tell you, without hesitation, that one of the very first lives he changed and empowered was mine. Throughout the weeks, months, and years of the aforementioned "dismantling and reassembly," Tim and I talked almost daily. He would share with me the day in the life of his journey; what he was toiling with, his struggles, his triumphs, his fears, and even his failures. I have to admit, I had never heard a man say the words, "I failed at that, but here's what I learned."

It was an honesty that I had never experienced before. Most of my conversations with other men, up to this point, revolved around football highlights, glory days, and local politics, but Tim and I were talking about real life stuff! Wives, kids, pain, love, fear and humility, to name a few. I also noticed more and more that there was an "iron sharpening iron" thing happening in our relationship. And, although we were side-by-side friends, there seemed to be a swath he was carving out in his journey that I was beginning to experience and benefit from. If I was struggling with an issue, he had already found it, named it, and conquered it in his journey. He not only cleared the path for me to name and conquer my challenges, but shined a light on the next stepping stone. As I look back, God and Tim were leading me through the basic principles of this book. As a result, Tim's swath has gotten wider and deeper. I am now equipped to empower other men, and they, others. As we all stand shoulder to shoulder and push onward, that path will continue to grow, all because of one man's weakness.

So who is Tim Mitchum? I could list credentials like author, college graduate, successful entrepreneur, musician, leader of men. I could say that he's a devoted Christian, friend, son, and brother. But what he really is, is a man who had enough guts to lose his life in order to find it, and then enough compassion and courage to share with us this blueprint of how he rebuilt it, so we don't spend our whole life guessing at how to do it. And he's my best friend.

Why should you read this book?

I spent most of my days as a boy in man's clothes, going through life's motions, only to wonder…what is my life adding up to? Questioning, asking "Am I enough? Enough of a father? Enough of a husband? Son? Friend? Christian? Employee? Or boss?" Can you relate? If you feel like you aren't measuring up, but not sure to what,

If you can't specifically describe the qualities of a true authentic man; if you feel like you have more to give, but don't know how, or, even if you just want some tools and information to becoming the Hero you were meant to be, you will find what you're looking for in the pages of this book.

The pages and chapters you are about to read will, at a minimum, give you an amazing perspective and barometer for you to live your life, but I think it will prove to be a game-changer. It will change how you look at life, it will help you identify behaviors and chains that need to be broken, and it will give you a blueprint to construct within yourself the man you always wanted to be but didn't know how to be. So, let me be the first to congratulate you on this significant milestone in your life. Not only will your life change, but you will change the lives of those around you for generations to come, and they theirs.

Robert Deitch
6/29/2011 Ankeny, Iowa

CONTENTS

INTRODUCTION

Hero is an interesting word. It gets thrown around in our society so easily that it tends to be diluted to the point that we have a hard time really defining what one is. In the best case scenario, we are confused about it. You can look it up in the dictionary and come up with several different things to consider. For instance, in the Merriam Webster dictionary, Hero is defined as the following:

- A mythological or legendary figure, often of divine descent, endowed with great strength or ability

- An illustrious warrior

- A man admired for his achievements and noble qualities

- One who shows great courage

These definitions, which are obviously correct, considering that they are in the dictionary, lack something of serious value to me. There is nothing compelling about them. There is nothing transformational about these definitions.

It takes less and less to be called a Hero nowadays, because of the simple lack of performance of everyone around us. We are longing for them so badly that we start calling anybody who does the right thing a Hero.

Firemen, for example, are a group that we tend to attach the term Hero to because if there is a *situation* that requires them to risk their lives, they will do it in the effort to save ours.

Soldiers are another example, and deserve the utmost respect for the service they give to protect our freedoms. They, too, may find themselves in a *situation* that requires them to risk their lives for the benefit of others.

Being a current resident of Iowa, I've had the privilege to witness the very first Medal of Honor given to a living recipient since the Vietnam War. It was very interesting to me to see Salvatore Giunta, who seemed uncomfortable with all the attention. He seemed to be very humbled and focused on the fact that even though he was receiving this honor, there were many others who deserved it more or as much as him.

Or, how about Chelsey Sullenberger, more commonly known as Captain Sully, the pilot of American Airlines' flight 1549? Shortly after takeoff from LaGuardia Airport, found himself in a *situation* that required him to use all his piloting skills, acquired over thousands of hours of flying, to successfully land the plane in the Hudson River, saving all 155 lives on board.

These are all examples of people we would easily label as Heroes in today's society, and rightfully so.

But what if the fireman only took the job to have a 3-day work week, and didn't do it to run into fires to save lives? What if the soldier signed up for the military for financial incentives, and not with the pure intention of risking his life on the front lines in war to protect our freedoms? And what if ol' Captain Sully was simply trying to save his own life by making the miraculous landing in the Hudson? Would we still consider these people heroes? The answer is YES, but in my book they are what we call "Situational Heroes."

There are endless examples of situational heroes; people who in the moment did their jobs, the right thing, or even risked their lives for the sake of another with zero benefit of their own, like Wesley Autrie, known as the "Subway Hero," who in 2007 jumped down onto the tracks to save Cameron Hollopeter, a 20 year-old film student who had suffered a seizure that caused him to lose his balance and fall into the path of a New York subway train.

Heroes yes, but let's redefine them as *situational* heroes, because they were Heroes only in what they did, not necessarily for who they were. Now let's take the rest of this book to learn about the "Transformational Hero," one who transforms lives through strategic focus, commitment, and investment of time into somebody else's future.

From this point on, when I refer to Heroes I'm talking about the Transformational Hero and not the Situational Hero. I'm way too lazy to type the word Transformational that many times.

So here's the deal. It's real simple. You need a Hero, I need a Hero, and we both need to be Heroes for our God, Wife, Significant Other, Family, Friends, Kids, and Community. The world is desperate for real Heroes to step up and strategically become these Heroes who literally change the world for generations beyond themselves. My goal is to share with you exactly how we can do that, step by step, so that when we come to the end of our lives, our momentum is so strong that it carries on for generations to come.

The brutal truth is this. You are already somebody's Hero. The real question is whether your actions are a contradiction to their vision of what that means, or an affirmation of it. Contradictions can destroy; affirmations will transform. Let's get on with becoming the Hero you are meant to be.

The Broken Mailbox

"I went looking for a Hero, but only found a man." Author Unknown

The following true story is the inspiration that gave me the vision for this book. I share it with you to give you greater understanding of what it looks like to completely miss the mark on becoming a real Hero so that we can steer clear of that tragic ending.

I told myself that today was the day, and I wouldn't wait any longer. I had let this go on long enough; 23 years to be exact. I was going to finally have the conversation that would start a new chapter in my life, that in my mind, would include a growing relationship with my BioDad (I'll explain that term later). I didn't know exactly why I decided that a specific Wednesday in April, 2010 would be the day that I finally confronted my BioDad and asked him THE question, but it was, and nothing was going to stop me.

After building up all the courage I could muster, I thought it would be best to take the Harley Davidson, and not the hatchback, to the impromptu meeting. I figured that if I took the motorcycle I could put on the garb that went along with it, like the leather jacket, bandana, boots, goggles, and grime from the road that would make me feel tougher on the outside, to cover up for the scared little boy on the inside. So there I was, all leathered up, headed down the highway to BioDad's house to ask him the question. I pulled off the highway and took the exit that would lead to my final destination. As I was driving down the road to his house, I started to question everything that I was doing. I continued to pray for strength, as I felt my leather bravado weakening with every block. I turned the corner and saw his house. With my hands firmly gripped on my extremely high handlebars or otherwise known as ape hangars, I started to reach for the clutch to slow down, but lost my nerve. I thought, *How am I going to actually go up and knock on his door?*

I twisted the throttle and went right by. I felt terribly weak, but I knew I wasn't going to give up. I just didn't know exactly how I was going to do it. So I went to the convenience store up the street and began to give myself a mental pep talk. *You can do this Tim. He is more afraid of you than you are of him.* I really wasn't sure about that one.

I started to pray. "God, I don't know how I am going to have the courage to walk up to that door and knock, so I need you to give it to me because I can't find it on my own."

So, after having a bottle of water and wasting as much time as I could reasonably excuse myself for, I got back on my Harley with a new strength and headed down the road. As I turned the corner I saw him outside at his mailbox, which was completely out of my plan, but obviously a prayer answered that I didn't have go up to the door and knock. Although I was grateful for that gift, it was enough of a change in plans to give me the excuse I needed to go ahead and throttle on by. I wouldn't go far this time, though. I started to laugh at myself, and God really laid on my heart that this is it. I turned around for my third approach. You would think that I was trying to land a 747 airplane on a little grass strip on the side of the mountain with the amount of attempts I made, but I finally was committed and at peace.

I eased off the throttle as I approached him as he was leaning over next to his mailbox. I came to a rolling stop, shut off the motorcycle, and while still sitting on it looked over at him. He slowly lifted his head just enough to see who it was before turning his attention back to the mailbox. I said, "Hey Doc, what's going on?"

He responded, "Where's your helmet?"

I thought, *Really, that's the first thing you have to say to your illegitimate child who just shows up out of nowhere; ask me where my helmet is?*

"I don't wear one," I said, and asked, "What happened to your mailbox?"

He replied, "Well, the snowplow truck decided they didn't like it very much and knocked it over during the last snow, and now that the snow has melted it no longer has any support to stand up on its own, so now I'm trying to get her put back up and braced correctly so I can get my mail again."

That was the beginning of the conversation that would change the direction of my life. But let's rewind a little, so you understand why I was at that mailbox.

I am what you call a bastard child. I am the child of an affair that happened between my mother, who was married, with two children at the time, and this guy I call BioDad, who was also married at the time, with six children. After my birth, it was pretty obvious to the guy who was married to my mother that I was not his child, considering he wasn't able to produce the sperm needed to create children; hence, my brother and sister, both older, were adopted. Within a year, my mother divorced this guy named Ron, who ended up moving 8 hours south, to Springfield Missouri, where we would see him once a year for a week, and he would actually work the whole week when we were there. My sister and brother and I would spend a lot of time picking up cans and finding things to do all day. We got the normal birthday and Christmas cards, but that pretty much sums up my relationship with him. There wasn't much to it. He remarried, to a woman who wasn't all that fond of his previous life; that was obvious, but I didn't know any different, and it was just the way it was.

Everything changed when I was 14. Two things happened that year. 1) Ron died of a massive heart attack on Christmas Eve, 1988, and 2) I was told that he wasn't really my biological father and that this other guy, who we'll call Doc, was. Big year in my life, to say the least. The passing of Ron didn't affect me much. I actually didn't know him all that well, and when we went to the funeral I remember thinking about how I have no idea who this guy is that they're describing. I even remember starting to cry and thinking, *Am I crying because I am sad, or am I crying because I think I am supposed to?* The "normal" reaction to losing a father may be extreme loss, sadness, and anger. But the truth is, I didn't feel like I really lost anything, because he was never there to lose.

On the other hand, I did find out about my NEW father, who was my REAL father, from my mom and sister, who sat me down on the flower-patterned couch to tell me who he was. I remember that it was a summer day, and I just couldn't figure out what was so serious that they both needed to talk to me. I thought for a brief moment that my sister had finally ratted me out about the water balloon incident at my 12th birthday party, but I was wrong. It was much bigger than that. My mom pretty much flat out said, "Timmy, Ron is not your real father. Your real father is this other guy." Who we will just call Doc.

I was so excited, and here's why. I knew this Doc guy, and I could actually reach him. Ron had always been 8 hours away, and distant in every way. But this guy I could get to; he had actually been my family physician since my birth. Even crazier, he delivered me, then physically handed me to Ron who obviously knew I wasn't his child. I'm still amazed to this day at the amount of arrogance it must have taken to do that. My mom decided to tell me for various reasons which are unimportant to this story, but the really exciting thing was that I finally had the "Hero" I was unknowingly longing for.

Up until that point, my life had felt clumsy. I was confused about how to act as a boy trying to become a man on his own. I didn't have the "why" answers to all of those normal questions you have as you begin the transition from boy to man, that I was looking for. Those unanswered questions and lack of concrete directions about life create serious frustration in a young man, and will eventually find an outlet, good or bad. That was all about to change.

I could finally get this guy who was my father and Hero to answer all these questions about life and give me the direction I needed. I would finally feel like life wasn't the burden it had been up to that point, because I would finally have the Captain to this thing called life, to teach me how to sail through any storm to reach my safe harbor.

I would have bet my life that from that moment on I would be busy with fishing trips, father-son banquets, Saturdays under the hood of a broken-down car, and on and on. It was almost as if in that moment I had envisioned this life of father and son blissfully skipping through man land together, hand in hand. One problem…

He was still married with 6 kids of his own, and his family didn't know anything about me, and wouldn't know anything about me, because it didn't really fit into his whole image as a perfect husband and father to the outside community.

So I kept my mouth shut, and for the next 23 years. I knew who he was, he knew who I was, but I didn't say a word. I continued to see him as my family physician for years, until I became angry at the fact that we still had to pay for treatment, even though in my mind I was doing him a huge favor and he really owed me. We would run into each other at the local gas station and he would try to avoid me by skirting out quicker than normal or taking the "not so direct" aisle to get out the door. There were lots of times at that gas station that I just said to myself, *Whatever*, and didn't even attempt to say "Hi," as it felt like I had to reintroduce myself to remind him who I was every time. It was very annoying and painful. Then there was this one time, when I was about 28, that brought myself, BioDad, BioDad's wife, and BioDad's daughter (my half sister) to a kitchen table all at once. I was selling stone veneer, the kind that would go on the outside of your house, for a local company when I got the call to go out and sell some stone to someone who had called in and was interested. When I saw the name of the person, I knew exactly who it was; my half-sister, BioDad's daughter. Because I had gotten so good at keeping this secret, I didn't think too much of it, except for the fact that I would finally get to know one of his kids. I had no idea that BioDad and his wife would be there to help her pick out the stone. So there I am standing in the driveway when BioDad's suburban pulls up. I wish I could describe the look on his face when he saw me and give it justice, but I'm sure that's impossible. Needless to say, he was shocked, but composed. We all sat down at the kitchen table to go over the details, which were the last things on my mind. I couldn't help but wonder what he was thinking in that moment.

Was he nervous? Was he thinking this may be the moment my whole world ends as I know it?

I wondered whether his wife noticed that we looked identical. I wondered if maybe his wife knew who I was from questions she asked which seemed a little odd, like, "Where are you from again? Where do you live now?" I mean, it wouldn't be the first time spouses had turned a blind eye to what they knew was going on in their marriage, and chose to do nothing, as opposed to having to create discomfort in the comfortable life they had been accustomed to. Maybe it was just my heightened sense of awareness of the incredibly odd situation. I did get a chance to witness how she ran the show and how he just sat there passively, letting her tell him what to do like a whipping boy. I kept thinking, *What if I just blurted out that your husband has been cheating on you for years and I am actually his son?* Would I be putting my commission in jeopardy? I laughed to myself inside, as I said nothing and treated the whole thing as a normal stone-selling situation. I kept the secret, he just sat there, I sold some stone, and everybody was happy.

When I pulled up to his mailbox on the Harley, I was really expecting a more of a HOLY COW response, considering this was the first time I had openly blended our two secret worlds, and it was in his driveway. After the initial pleasantries about how his mailbox got broken, I put the kickstand down on the gravel shoulder, took off the heavy leather jacket that was my emotional armor up to that point, slid off my gloves and stepped off of the motorcycle. For the next 20 minutes, I helped him fix his broken mailbox. We talked about proper bracing, the correct placement of nails—I personally would have used screws—the tools needed, and I held boards in place to watch him take what seemed like 5 million swings to get one nail in. I'm serious that there was a moment when I thought, *If he doesn't start swinging that hammer like a man I am going to take it from him and do it myself.* It was the first moment in my life when I was really frustrated with the way my "father" was doing something. I started laughing to myself about feeling that way, and decided to let him take all the time he needed to get it nailed, because I wasn't here to help him fix his mailbox, although it seems I had somehow migrated into this situation.

After 20 minutes, we ran out of nails. He looked up at me and said, "Well, thanks for stopping by. I have to run and get some more supplies, so thanks again." I pulled out a verbal lasso to catch him before he tried to sprint down the driveway back to safety and said, "You know I didn't come here to help you fix your mailbox, right?"

He said, "Ya, I kind of figured that."

Now we were at the moment I had been waiting for, for the last 23 years. The moment where I could flat out ask him whether or not he wanted to have a relationship with me, period.

In the months prior to this defining moment in my life, I had been experiencing an unusual amount of sporadic anger toward him. I wasn't sure what I was going to say to him when I finally got up the courage, but I knew I had to confront this situation head-on, so I could move on with my life and let it go. I needed to be the man, because he obviously wasn't going to come to me. I needed to take back control of my life, and no longer be a victim of what I thought he had done to me. So I started praying.

I had been praying for weeks about what would I say that would accomplish the following: 1) Make it clear what I was talking about him being my BioDad, 2) make it so he wasn't able to weasel out of answering the question, and 3) make it so he had to start off-balance, and couldn't fabricate something. I couldn't come up with it on my own. Although a majority of my income is made from getting people to take action from reading words through some kind of direct marketing, I couldn't figure out what to say on my own. And then one day in prayer it came to me as if God was at a chalkboard in the front of my mind writing out what to say so perfectly that it would accomplish all three of those goals.

I looked up at him, as I sat on my steel horse of man strength and said, "You know, I have been thinking about this moment for the last 23 years. The day that we would finally have this conversation and what it was that I would say to you. But that fact is, Doc, I could never figure out what it was that I would say, so I'm going to go ahead and let you start."

Enter the sound of crickets. I swore that after I said that I would not say another word until he started to finally speak. I would still be there to this day if he hadn't opened his lips to show me exactly what kind of a man he was, and *boy* did he.

Because he was 78 years old, I figured that for the most part I would be getting into an adult conversation with the "Hero" I had imagined. I really thought that the first words out of his mouth would be something like, "Tim, I am sorry that I wasn't there for you. I made the choice to protect myself first at your expense. I would like to start over, and with your forgiveness begin a new relationship with you while I still can." That would have been great, but what ended up coming out of his mouth was more closely related to what you might expect from a 10 year old who just got caught stealing candy bars with his friends at the gas station.

With his voice cracking and his eyes staring up and to the left he replied, "Well, your Mother wanted a child, so I gave her one, and I didn't want my family to know, because I was trying to protect you, as I didn't think they would accept you, and blah, blah, blah, blah, blah, blah."

Something happened in that moment that changed my life. I remember everything else he said, but it really added up to nothing. It was more about what he didn't say. And what changed was that I went from having a certain amount of anger towards him to being completely sad for him. I gained this powerful little emotion that had been really hard for me to come by until that point, called "compassion." I realized that my expectation was to finally find my Hero, and when I got there and put him in a position that he had to show who he was, I found nothing but a child stuck in a 78-year-old man's body. I realized that he had no idea what it was to be a man, and couldn't even comprehend what it would take to be a Hero, but also realized that it most likely wasn't his fault, because he didn't have anybody to show him. It also became very clear to me that he was going to die eventually, with a regret that I cannot even fathom, of knowing that he wasn't living an authentic life during his short time here on earth that transformed lives of those around him. He lived for himself, he lived with un-reconciled secrets, he lived for praise at work, and that would eventually lead to a lonely death, regardless of how many people showed up to his funeral.

As my mind began to tune out his self-preserving babble, I had a vision that is the reason you are reading this today. The vision was twofold; 1) I would never be at the end of my life the way he finds himself, and 2) I would do whatever I could to create something that showed others how to become the Hero they are meant to be and the world deserves. One who at the end of their life has more momentum than in the beginning. One who lives UP and not down, but especially not level. One who strategically transforms lives around them and leaves a legacy that continues to positively affect lives for generations to follow.

I had no idea how I was going to do this, because I was less than a Hero myself, in many ways, but I drew a line in the sand that day and have been living UP every since. I want to share with you this step-by-step Heroes Blueprint that has changed my life and the lives of those around me, and has the power to change your life and transform the lives of those around you in this journey to living and ending your life as a Transformational Hero, and not merely just a man, and certainly not a boy stuck in a 78-year-old body.

Step 1:

Recognizing the Need for Heroes

"Character is caught, not taught" *Author Unknown*

Not long ago, I was invited to be a fly on the wall at a meeting that took place at a little coffee shop here in Des Moines, Iowa. I wasn't even really sure why I was invited, except that my good friend and mentor, Ed Nichols, who was putting it on, said I should be there. I was currently involved with and facilitating multiple men's groups aimed at showing guys how to live authentically and become men who liked the reflection they saw in the mirror. I thought this meeting must be something along the same lines.

When I got there, everyone was handing out their business cards, which always makes me a little uncomfortable because I don't have a card. For a moment, I felt like I should have a card to be important, but then I realized there isn't a card that exists that could do that for me. I'm content with the fact, that finally, after years of battling, I have gotten to a level of awareness that helps me see clearly that my identity has nothing to do with my business card, but rather who I am without it. After settling into my spot, I was handed a sheet of paper that listed all the groups represented. I think there were 16 different groups, and each had been given a 5-minute window to talk about what they did, or who they were and what they needed. When I heard that they were going to tell us what they needed, I immediately assumed this was going to be a fundraising event, but boy was I wrong.

The 16 non-profit groups included faith-based organizations along with secular ones. There were representatives from the Caucasian, African-American, and Hispanic communities. Some of the groups were of national affiliation, and others exclusive to Iowa. So it was a really interesting mix of folks, all in one room, looking to tell us who they are and what they needed. The first organization to speak was a group that went by the name Wildwood Hills Ranch, a ranch set on 400 acres of beautiful Madison County, Iowa land. Same place "The Bridges of Madison County" was filmed. They provide ongoing learning opportunities for at-risk and neglected children who come from severely impoverished, low-income families, both in the rural and inner city neighborhoods across the State of Iowa and surrounding border communities, all in a ranch setting with fishing, canoeing, and camping, among other activities. Their biggest need? 450 men to volunteer to help out with the summer camps.

Next up was Big Brothers and Big Sisters of Iowa. The thing that really blew me away is that they have a school-based program that's a commitment of only 30 minutes a week. I couldn't even come up with an excuse for 30 minutes a week. Can you imagine how much life you could breathe into a kid just investing 30 minutes a week? Up until that point I didn't even realize that they had a school-based program. Their biggest need was men to get matched with boys. Currently there was a waiting list of about 95 boys. The YMCA was up next. They have a project called the Mentoring project that's in desperate need of men to come along for a kid who needs some simple life direction, encouragement, and skills that will help them get to the next level in life. After all 16 of these organizations had completed their spiel, I looked down at my notes and realized that every one of these groups except one said their biggest need was men. Men to volunteer to spend time invested in another child or young adult. I'm not talking about a lifetime commitment. There were many weekend, hourly, and short-term opportunities that I had no idea about. I'm involved with the YMCA project, but am definitely going to be getting involved with the Wildwood Hills Ranch deal. I mean, who doesn't want to go canoeing, fishing, and camping, all the while getting the reward of mentoring another?

You don't have to be at a meeting in Des Moines, Iowa to see the need for Heroes in our society. Just open your eyes, and you will see divorce rates creeping close to 50% that make you wonder if marriage is really a commitment or just a more expensive form of dating; something that may or may not work out. Or how about extra-marital affairs? I've personally been aware of more than 10 extra-marital affairs in the last 3 years, that are happening in the workplace, in the church, and everywhere in between. Some end in divorce; some work through it and start the healing process, which is a long road. I see desperate daughters, who never had a Hero to model how a man should love a woman. No one to show them how they should expect to be treated. I watch these young boys, who never had a Hero teach them what it means to be a man, try and figure it out on their own, creating confusion, hurting others, and making huge mistakes. All these outcomes are a direct correlation to the lack of Transformational Heroes in our society. You stick a Hero in there, and you have a strategic modeling of respectful love between a man and a woman, so these daughters will settle for nothing less than that same respect in a man they date or eventually marry. You see sons taking the high road in life because they have been strategically invested to eliminate the confusion we boys have as we grow up about what it means to be a man, and who we try and prove that to.

You stick a Hero into any one of these situations and you eliminate the fallout.

I was reading a quote the other day by a guy named Frederick Douglass who said, "It is better to build strong children than to repair broken men."

I really thought about this for a while, because I was wondering who was going to be building these strong children if you forget about repairing the broken men?

I'm glad somebody chose to ignore that quote and invest in me as a broken man, because my life has changed through this Heroes Blueprint. I have been living for and will end my life as the Transformational Hero who takes a lot of guys with me. A lot of guys who go out and breathe life into others and show them the Heroes Blueprint. And that will not only repair broken men, but will also raise mighty children.

Do you have what it takes? I promise that no matter where you're at in your life, you can do it. All you have to do is commit to it. Are you man enough for that? The fact you are reading this tells me that a cape will probably fit you just fine.

Questions to Think About

- Who have been Heroes in your life, up to this point?

- What was it about them that made you think of them as Heroes?

- Think about any missed opportunities for Heroes in you life. (An example would be my BioDad.)

- Think about any opportunities that you may have missed to be a Hero.

- Think about who may be looking at you now as a Hero.
  - What about your life affirms a positive vision of a Hero to them?
  - What about your life confuses those watching as to what a Hero should be?

- Think about any organizations that come to mind in your area that may be a place for you to get involved.

- What is the most important thing you are taking away from this chapter?

Step 2:
LIVE FOR YOUR LAST BREATH

"Begin with the end in mind." Stephen Covey

Stephen Covey wrote a bestselling book, *The 7 Habits of Highly Successful People*, in which he talks about habit #2, which is *Begin with the end in mind*. I love this concept. Pretty much every great invention, idea, and life-changing product was created this way.

Even the most simple tasks we do on a regular basis comes from this concept. Take, for instance, if we want to pick up a glass of water and take a drink. We do not think, "Okay, I need to alert my nervous system to move my arm the proper distance to reach the glass, and then I need to tell it to make sure my hands grips it appropriately, and then lift it up towards my mouth, and then open my mouth," etc. I think you get my point. What we do is think, "I want a drink of water," and everything starts working in a collaborative effort to make that happen without us thinking about it, at least not consciously.

The second step in the Heroes Blueprint is to begin with our last breath in mind. Literally with your last breath in mind. You have to visualize this feeling intensely, so that you can understand what you need to do to make it the most fulfilling breath you ever take.

For me, when I started down this path of identifying and creating this blueprint, I envisioned my last breath as being one of complete satisfaction, surrounded by people who loved me for the way I loved and served them. It will feel very light, with no regret, and I will leave with a smile on my face, knowing that I have led the life of a Hero that will continue to transform lives for many generations to come.

The best way I have found to start with the end in mind is to to take the time to create a personal mission statement. What I have found is that my personal mission statement has become an accountability partner of sorts. When I feel as if I am getting off track or something is out of whack in my life, I can usually go back to my personal mission statement, identify where I'm falling short, and correct it very quickly, so that I stay on track to enjoy that last breath.

There isn't a right or wrong way to create your personal mission statement, because everyone is different and unique in their own way. I've worked with men who wrote out simple bullet points and others who wrote out very elaborate descriptive statements that were very detailed. Regardless, your goal is to identify how you want to live your life, who you want to be, what you want to accomplish, and how you want to accomplish it.

Some will argue that your personal mission statement is something that does not change over time. I personally believe that it is something that you can amend over time to reflect the new understanding and wisdom you gain along the way, but, fundamentally, it stays congruent to its original focus. Let me give you an example that may help you start to develop one of your own. We'll break it down into pieces, so you can see the thought and process behind it.

Here is my personal mission statement:

To be a great man of God who creates wealth, and with this wealth provides means to those in need, always in His name. And in doing so, I motivate, inspire, and lead others, always leaving them better than before I met them, and always leaving them with a taste of the Holy Spirit on their lips. I will finish strong, with increasing momentum as a great lover, a great fighter, and a great finisher for Christ, who with a pure heart, clear conscience, and sincere faith leaves a wake of righteousness behind for others to follow.

Let's take the first piece:

To be a great man of God who creates wealth, and with this wealth provides means to those in need, always in His name.

Okay, so in the first part what I'm identifying is that I want to live my life obediently to God. I use the term "Great Man" to reflect being obedient to His word. This obedience to Him will make me the great husband, father, friend, etc., that I aim to be.

Wealth, for me, represents two things. 1) That I have money to live my life free from financial constraints that keep me from being flexible to do what I feel called to do. 2) That the things I create have tremendous value, whether it be books, speeches, audio programs, or whatever, and they find their way to those in need of them. I also want to have a healthy relationship with money, understanding that it is simply given to me to use for God's good, and I will always be a good steward of this gift, investing it wisely, giving it away responsibly, and tithing faithfully.

Let's take a look at the second piece:

And in doing so, I motivate, inspire and lead others, always leaving them better than before I met them, and always leaving them with a taste of the Holy Spirit on their lips.

In the second part, what I'm identifying is how I want to use my natural gift of speaking, motivation, inspiration, and leadership to obtain this wealth, financial stability, and in general live a more fulfilled life by staying in my sweet spot of talents. I add "to always leave them better than before I met them" to remind myself of the struggles I've had in the past, and battle to this day, with being reckless with my words and causing others unnecessary pain to cover up my own insecurities. I end this section with "leaving them with a taste of the Holy Spirit on their lips" to remind myself that I am not a pastor, nor do I want to ever debate about faith or religion. My best witness to others is by planting seeds of faith in them through my actions, sharing my life, and how God has transformed me, in which God cultivates in his time.

And finally, the last section:

I will finish strong, with increasing momentum as a great lover, a great fighter, and a great finisher for Christ, who with a pure heart, clear conscience, and sincere faith leaves a wake of righteousness behind for others to follow.

In this last piece I'm saying that at the end of my life I want to finish so strong that the momentum from my life will be increasing, regardless of my death. I want to have loved well, fought aggressively for what I believed in and against what is unjust, and finished well. In order to do these things authentically, I will need a pure heart; one that is devoted to serving something greater than myself. I will need a clear conscience, reflecting a life of integrity and reconciliation. And I will need a sincere faith that exhibits trust and obedience. When all of these things are done to the best of my ability, I fully expect a wake or trail of my life left behind that models something worth following.

I could have just as easily bulleted-pointed that same personal mission statement and it would have looked something like this:

- Be a faithful follower of Christ

- A strategic husband, father, and friend

- A provider, financially and emotionally

- Be financially independent

- Create things in my work that add value to others' lives

- Tithe faithfully, and more every year

- Look for opportunities to be charitable with money or time

- Choose my words carefully to breathe life into others, and not the opposite

- Focus on earning, through my sweet spot of talents

- Live a life that plants seeds of faith through my actions

- And on and on.

It really doesn't matter how you do it, but it does matter that you do. Going through this process and creating your own personal mission statement will give you a great sense of freedom and direction. You will have that mini-accountability partner to keep your emotions and actions in check. And, over time, you may find that you want to add or tweak it a little bit, because you are growing in certain areas of your life, and are getting wiser. I have no doubt that this will be the case, and when you look back on your original personal mission statement you will be able to see how much you have grown and how you have narrowed your focus to what truly matters in your life.

Creating Your Own Personal Mission Statement

Go ahead and start this process of creating your own mission statement. I've put the examples from this chapter of mine below just to give you a little direction, but remember that you can do it any way you want. A question I've found valuable to ask yourself to get started is this:

"If you were able to overhear a conversation of someone who knew you describing to someone who didn't know you, about who you were as a person. What would you want to hear?"

My written example:

To be a great man of God who creates wealth, and with this wealth provides means to those in need, always in His name. And in doing so, I motivate, inspire, and lead others, always leaving them better than before I met them, and always leaving them with a taste of the Holy Spirit on their lips. I will finish strong, with increasing momentum as a great lover, a great fighter, and a great finisher for Christ, who with a pure heart, clear conscience, and sincere faith leaves a wake of righteousness behind for others to follow.

My bulleted example:

- *Be a faithful follower of Christ*
- *A strategic husband, father, and friend*
- *A provider, financially and emotionally*
- *Be financially independent*
- *Create things in my work that add value to others' lives*
- *Tithe faithfully, and more every year*
- *Look for opportunities to be charitable with money or time*

- *Choose my words carefully, to breathe life into others and not the opposite*
- *Focus on earning through my sweet spot of talents*
- *Live a life that plants seeds of faith through my actions*
- *And on and on…*

Yours:

_____

_____

_____

_____

_____

_____

_____

_____

_____

_____

_____

_____

_____

_____

Step 3:

COMMIT TO BECOMING A HERO

"Do the thing and you will have the power." Ralph Waldo Emerson

Nothing in this world is accomplished without someone first taking some kind of action. Before there is any kind of physical action, there has to be some level of commitment to put that action into motion. The process of unleashing your inner Hero and becoming the man your God, significant other, wife, kids, family, community and world deserves starts with making the commitment to the process of becoming this Transformational Hero.

This process is not for the faint at heart. If you are a "maybe" man, then this will be your gut check, and become an unbelievably powerful thing for you. The Hero doesn't allow himself an "out," but instead commits to the process, because he has already started with the end in mind and realize there will be nothing greater than fulfilling that vision.

If you are already one of those men who commits to something, and follows through and finishes, I admire you. It took me many years to start to become one, and I still work on it intentionally every day. It wasn't something I saw on a daily basis, nor was it modeled for me, growing up. I remember very vividly that one of the first examples of what I would call an example of someone committing to something that wasn't easy to do and then following through, was in my mid-twenties, by my great friend, Troy Salazar.

It was during the muggy part of the Iowa summer, at the end of July, heading into August. At this time around Iowa, we tend to think of the world-renowned Iowa State Fair, where you can literally get almost anything deep-fat fried on a stick. I love the Fair, and usually head out by myself a couple of times in addition to meeting up with friends, going to concerts, and just flat out people-watching. There are lots of mullets, interesting outfits (to say the least), and the best guinea grinders anywhere.

But a few weeks prior, a neighbor of mine asked if I would help him build a retaining wall to hold up some loose dirt threatening to spill into the garage and on the driveway. I'd been selling landscape materials, and worked for a landscape contractor to put myself through college, so I had all the skills needed to be the perfect victim of a neighbor's landscaping project. I did not want to do it, but felt like I should, because this neighbor had taught me how to sail a little boat I inherited from my grandfather, years before. I felt like it was an opportunity to maybe return the favor, although my selfish nature was weighing how much better of a deal he was getting out of this trade than I was. He got to go sailing, I got to dig in the dirt.

I mentioned to Troy that I had this project to help build my neighbor's retaining wall that I was dreading, and he said, without hesitation, "If you need help, I'll help."

Yeah, okay, I'd said that exact phrase right before I usually started fabricating future excuses to get me out of something many times before. I didn't really think that much of it until I called Troy and said, "Hey we're going to build that wall this Saturday, so if you're still able to help, that would be great."

He replied, "I'll be there."

Deep down, I truly believe I was thinking, *Troy is really going to drag this one out and come up with an excuse the very last minute, because, after all, it was the end of July in Iowa, which means 100 degrees with 100% humidity, he wasn't getting paid, and it was actually helping someone he did not really even know.* None of that made sense to me in the first place, but when the morning came to start, Troy showed up with work boots and gloves in hand. I remember saying to him when he pulled into my driveway, "I can't believe you showed up."

He calmly replied, "I said I would help, so I am here to help."

We ended up working all day, on the hottest day of the year, to help build this retaining wall, which, by the way, is still standing. I sometimes drive by it to remind myself of the lesson I learned that day from my good buddy Troy. He committed to helping me, and he showed up when at that point in my life I might not have for him.

Building that wall was terrible physically, but Troy and I became closer that day through the sweat and pain. I had been blessed by Troy's commitment and follow-through when he really didn't have any tangible gain from it. It was a simple lesson that I will never forget.

The commitment you're making to becoming a Hero is a lot bigger than a Saturday building a wall with your buddy, but it has three very similar traits.

1. Commit

2. Show up

3. Follow through

Saying "NO" is also a commitment, because you are committed to doing nothing. I actually have a buddy who says no to everything, and I respect him more for not being a maybe man and disappointing later.

Make the commitment today, and let the process start; that will transform your life and the lives of others around you. Or you could just say NO and continue down whatever path you're on, which is fine, but whatever you do, don't say "maybe" because that word leads to disappointment, lack of direction, and confusion, which ultimately falls short of anything great.

Simple Action Step

I want you to say the following statement below as a symbol of your commitment. You will be amazed at how just saying it changes something inside:

I commit today to becoming a Hero who transforms my life and the lives of those around me, and I will take the necessary steps to make this happen.

Step 4:
START THE GUTTING PROCESS

"Your past does not define your future." Tony Robbins

The first time I heard this, I was driving along listening to a Tony Robbins CD. I remember thinking, *Whew... I'm sure glad to hear that.* It wasn't like I had committed some terrible crime or spent years in jail or anything, but I certainly had my fair share of personal and professional failures that weighed heavily on me, even if I didn't want to admit it on the outside. As guys, we're pretty good at compartmentalizing our emotions and only letting the ones that we think make us appear strong, successful, or with it, show to others.

For better or worse, we are *absolutely* shaped by the experiences we had in the home, growing up, and the choices we have made. We are definitely products of the past, but not prisoners of it. And the truth is that unless we deal with our past, we will not be able to truly move forward into the future as authentic men on their way to becoming Heroes. I think Socrates lays it out very well when he said at his heresy trial that, "*The unexamined life is not worth living.*"

Before I started this gutting process, which took me deep into examining my past, life to me felt like I was running a marathon in work boots, in the mud. That's the only way I can accurately describe it. Even though I appeared to be moving on the outside, it felt very heavy and laboring on the inside. It was like our grandparents always saying, "Walking uphill both ways."

I didn't really know what the next step was, considering there wasn't a blueprint for me to follow. I decided to do what Socrates suggested, and went into examination mode.

I signed up for this course my church was offering, called "Christ Life." It was designed to take you all the way back to the beginning of your life and dissect every pivotal situation and feeling that was associated with it, so that you could move past any negative things that kept you in bondage. You met with a group of people from various backgrounds, who all spilled their life stories to each other. It was not easy, and at this point in my life I had zero compassion, but I managed to get through it because of the commitment I'd made, that you a reader of this book, have made.

I ended up being the only one left out of 6 people who started in my group. Sometimes I think I ended up being placed there to facilitate the facilitator, but there were three things I ended up getting out of this process that were priceless. 1) I did learn a lot about some of my own issues, and was able to forgive myself and others, and to move on, although not yet to my Bio Dad, 2) I learned how to listen, and 3) I realized how much effect words have on others' lives.

I couldn't believe the effect that a little joke made at another's expense could have on that person's life. What I would have laughed off had massive negative impacts on others' lives. They would carry it with them forever, almost like having a recording in their head repeating it to them over and over again. It was painful to listen to, because it brought to light that I had been the negative recording in many others' heads. There is a scripture now that I often turn to to remind me of the effect my words can have on others.

"Reckless words pierce like a sword, but the tongue of the wise brings healing." (Proverbs 12:18)

I'm not always successful at holding back my reckless words, but I'm now more successful than not, and I will always try to better my average. This Scripture definitely helps.

It also became very clear to me that in my ignorant attempt to prove my manhood as a young man through taking advantage of desperate daughters, I had left a canyon of hurt and emptiness in these women as well as in myself. It was painful to experience reality, but needed in order to begin living authentically on the way to becoming a Hero.

There were three phases to this "Christ Life" process. I went through two of them, and really got a lot of value out of the process. I didn't go through the third phase, because they didn't offer it anywhere near to where I was living. That was step 1 in this gutting process, and I highly recommend it if you have somewhere near you where it is offered.

The second thing I did that had the greatest impact, so far, was taking a course called "The Quest for Authentic Manhood." The basic premise of this course was that we men have no stinking idea of what it truly means to be a man, and this confusion creates big problems in this world. I knew that for sure, considering the situation with my BioDad. Not only did that affect me, but his failure as a man ultimately affected his life as well.

Robert Lewis, who authors this Quest for Authentic Manhood course, makes five big promises to be delivered in the course.

1. You will have a clear definition of manhood.

2. You will develop new manhood language.

3. You will make significant personal discoveries about yourself.

4. You will make new friends who are pursuing a common goal.

5. You will have your own personalized Manhood Plan for achieving authentic manhood.

The first one sounds fairly simple, right? A clear definition of manhood? That's what I thought, until I tried to define what a real man was, and couldn't. If you think it's that easy, just take a moment, define it for yourself, and see how clear the definition is that you come up with. And then number 5 really stuck out to me as well. A real Manhood Plan! Wow! That sounded like exactly what I needed; a plan!

Robert Lewis goes deeply into the wounds we have as men in this world, and offers strategies to effectively deal with and move past them.

This Quest course is crucial to your success as a man, and a pivotal step in The Heroes Blueprint. I now facilitate this course for other guys, and I can't tell you how awesome it is to see the changes that are taking place in their lives.

Another really good tool to offer you at this point is a book I read in between the Christ Life and Quest courses. The book was *The Secret Life of the Soul*, by Keith Miller. This book helped me understand how, as children, we start to construct personality around how to protect ourselves from pain, make us feel adequate, intelligent, and/ or more honest than we actually are. This constructed personality, as he calls it, eventually keeps us from living an authentic life that leads to authentic self-esteem.

The gutting process is one that at some level you will continue for the rest of your life. It may seem daunting at first, but I assure you that it will be one of the most exhilarating things you do in your life. A perfect example of this is that the first group of The Quest for Authentic Manhood course that I facilitated met for 27 weeks straight, and we nearly had 100% attendance. At the end the men were extremely anxious to start going through a second phase. How is that possible? Well, when you're becoming a better man, it becomes addictive, because you see the changes in you, and how those changes affect every other area in your life positively. This is not an overnight process, but it's not something to fear. You will love it.

Heroes are constantly learning how to become more effective by getting rid of emotional baggage that slows us down or keeps us from performing at our best. It's a never-ending process that may feel like a gutting at first, but will eventually just take little tweaks here and there to dump the junk that's keeping us from living out our best life.

Courses to Investigate

I'm going to add these websites to the resources in the back of the book, but I wanted to add them here, too. As you know, these are the two courses that really started the gutting process that has freed me up in many areas of my life.

If you feel like, or know, that you have deep hurts from some past experiences, I would recommend starting with Christ Life. If you feel like you've had a pretty "normal" life, without serious wounds that you know of, then I would go straight to the Quest for Authentic Manhood course. Both will benefit you tremendously.

1. The Quest For Authentic Manhood website,
    http://www.mensfraternity.com
2. Christ Life Course website, http://www.christlifesolution.com

Step 5:
IDENTIFYING YOUR KRYPTONITE

"Never saw off the branch you are on,
unless you are being hanged from it." Stanislaw Lec

I'm fairly certain that if you're reading this, you already know exactly what Kryptonite is, but for those of who don't, I will give you the exact definition, according to Wikipedia:

Kryptonite is the ore form of a fictional element from the Superman mythos. It is one of the few things that can injure or kill Superman.

Originating in the Superman radio show series, the material is usually shown as having been created from the radioactive remains of Superman's native planet, Krypton, (which coincidentally shares its name with the real-life element, Krypton), and generally has detrimental effects on Superman and other Kryptonians. The name "kryptonite" covers a variety of forms of the substance, but usually refers to the most common "green" form.

In modern speech, the word kryptonite has become a synonym for Achilles' heel, the one weakness of an otherwise invulnerable hero.

It used to be painful for me, as a kid, watching Superman being held at bay by Lex Luthor, or some other criminal who had access to this green substance that could stop Superman in his tracks. It was frustrating to know how powerful Superman could be if he could just get away from the green stuff. It took away his powers and made him as normal as the next guy.

I like how Kryptonite is described as the Achilles Heel in the definition, the one weakness of an otherwise invulnerable hero.

Chances are you have already had some thoughts run through your mind that might be identifying some of your Kryptonite. Those things that keep you from:

1. Doing what you know is right

2. Saying what you should

3. Refraining from what you shouldn't say

4. Or acting in the appropriate way

No matter how much gutting we go through, there are going to be things that we constantly struggle with that literally take away our powers to be effective towards our goal of being the Transformational Hero. The gutting process is meant to become a habit that we continue throughout our life, at different stages, to make sure we continue to identify these things, and keep them in check, if not rid ourselves of them.

When I first went through this step, it became glaringly obvious to me that my top 3 out of what felt like hundreds were the following:

1. Pride

2. Self Control

3. Fear of What Other People Think (Social Phobia)

Pride kept me from being able to say, "I don't know," which in turn kept me from learning a lot about a lot of things. I was unable to humble myself enough to learn from others, because my pride was such a powerful force inside of me, built to protect my own insecurities and to hide any signs of weakness. Pride isn't necessarily always a bad thing, but for me, personally, it was. It didn't come from a healthy origin, and I still struggle with it today, but less than I used to. Kryptonite.

The lack of self control revealed itself in me through my words. Have you ever found yourself saying in your head over and over again, "Don't say it, don't say it, don't say it, it's not important, it will only hurt them, it's not worth it, don't say it," and then two seconds later you let the words vomit out of your mouth as you watch the other person's face turn to either one of pain or anger? Yeah, me too, LOTS.

Immediately after vomiting the words we tried to persuade ourselves not to say, the onslaught of guilt, embarrassment, and shame hits us like a freight train. Most of the time, it starts hitting us with the very first syllable that we let slip out, and if one syllable gets out, all of the syllables get out. Kryptonite.

And finally, for me the last one of my top 3 Kryptonites is fearing what other people think. I used to call this the fear of failure, until I realized that I wasn't actually afraid of failing, I was afraid of what others would *think* about me failing. That may seem like a no-brainer, but it was really a big moment for me to authentically understand this to be the truth. There is actually a clinical name given to this fear. It's called "Social Phobia." I might not have it to the extent that it's clinical, but it was certainly paralyzing in my life at times. Kryptonite. I could probably write a whole book about that, but I will spare you and me the pain.

My mom probably said it best one time, when she looked me square in the eye and said, "Tim, people don't spend that much time thinking about you. They're too busy worrying about themselves". They don't spend that much time thinking about your failures, either, so don't let that keep you from sticking your neck out there to make a change in your life that will lead to great things. And remember what Ben Franklin said about failing, "I didn't fail the test, I just found 100 ways of doing it wrong." We certainly don't think of him as a failure now do we?

Chances are, you already know some of the things that keep you from being effective and take away your powers to positively affect someone else; your Kryptonite. If you don't, you surely would have had some of them being revealed through the gutting process. If you're still completely lost about what some of your Kryptonite might be, I've listed 49 qualities of Christ. No matter what your faith or lack of faith is, it's hard to argue against Christ being a pretty good role model. He really is the ultimate transformational Hero, when you think about it. As you read down this list of qualities, you will find yourself identifying either positively or negatively to certain ones, and the ones that scream at you will be the ones you might think about writing down and working on.

Take the time to rate yourself by checking one of the boxes in the table to the left of each of the 49 qualities. Below you will find the explanation of what each box means.

49 Qualities of Christ

NW=Needs Work

NS=Not Sure

AM=Already Mastered

NW	NS	AM	
☐	☐	☐	**1. Alertness** vs. unawareness

Being aware of the physical and spiritual events taking place around me, so that I can have the right responses to them.

"But after I have been raised, I will go before you to Galilee." (*Mark 14:28*)

☐ ☐ ☐ **2. Attentiveness** vs. unconcern

Showing the worth of a person by giving undivided attention to his words and emotions.

"For this reason we must pay much closer attention to what we have heard, lest we drift away from it." (*Hebrews 2:1*)

☐ ☐ ☐ **3. Availability** vs. self-centeredness

Adjusting my personal responsibilities around the needs of those who I am serving.

"For I have no one else of kindred spirit who will genuinely be concerned for your welfare." (*Phillipians 2:20*)

NW   NS   AM

☐   ☐   ☐   **4. Boldness** vs. fearfulness

Confidence that what I have to say or do is true and right and just in the sight of God.

"And now, Lord take note of their threats, and grant that Thy bondservant may speak Thy word with all confidence." (Acts 4:29)

☐   ☐   ☐   **5. Cautiousness** vs. rashness

Knowing how important right timing is in accomplishing right actions.

"Also it is not good for a person to be without knowledge, and he who makes haste with his feet errs." (Proverbs 19:2)

☐   ☐   ☐   **6. Compassion** vs. indifference

Investing whatever is necessary to heal the hurts of others.

"But whoever has the world's goods, and beholds his brother in need and closes his heart against him, how does the love of God abide in him?" (1 John 3:17)

☐   ☐   ☐   **7. Contentment** vs. covetousness

Realizing that God has provided everything I need for my present happiness.

"And if we have food and covering, with these we shall be content." (1 Timothy 6:8)

NW   NS   AM

☐   ☐   ☐   **8. Creativity** vs. underachievement

Applying God's wisdom and practical insights to a need or task.

"And do not be conformed to this world, but be transformed by the renewing of your mind, that you may prove what the will of God is, that which is good and acceptable and perfect." (Romans 12:2)

☐   ☐   ☐   **9. Decisiveness** vs. double-mindedness

The ability to finalize difficult decisions based on the will and ways of God.

"But if any of you lacks wisdom, let him ask God, who gives to all men generously and without reproach, and it Will be given to him." (James 1:5)

☐   ☐   ☐   **10. Deference** vs. rudeness

Limiting my freedom to speak and act in order not to offend the taste of others.

"It is good not to eat meat or to drink wine, or to do anything by which your brother stumbles." (Romans 14:21)

☐   ☐   ☐   **11. Dependability** vs. inconsistency

Fulfilling what I consented to do, even if it means unexpected sacrifice.

"In whose eyes a reprobate is despised, but who honors those who fear the lord; He swears to his own hurt, and does not change." (Psalm 15:4)

NW   NS   AM

☐   ☐   ☐   **12. Determination** vs. faintheartedness

Purposing to accomplish God's goals in God's timing, regardless of the opposition.

"I have fought the good fight, I have finished the course, I have kept the faith; in the future there is laid up for me the crown of righteousness, which the Lord, the righteous Judge, will award to me on that day; and not only to me, but also to all who have loved His appearing." (2 Timothy 4:7-8)

☐   ☐   ☐   **13. Diligence** vs. slothfulness

Visualizing each task as a special assignment from the Lord and using all my energies to accomplish it.

"Whatever you do, do your work heartily, as for the Lord rather than for men." (Colossians 3:23)

☐   ☐   ☐   **14. Discernment** vs. judgment

The God-given ability to understand why things happen to others and to me.

"But the Lord said to Samuel, 'Do not look at his appearance or at the height of his stature, because I have rejected him; for God sees not as man sees, for man looks at the outward appearance, but the Lord looks at the heart." (1 Samuel 16:7)

NW   NS   AM

☐   ☐   ☐   **15. Discretion** vs. simplemindedness

The ability to avoid words, actions, and attitudes which could result in undesirable consequences.

"The prudent sees the evil and hides himself, but the naive go on, and are punished for it." *(Proverbs 22:3)*

☐   ☐   ☐   **16. Endurance** vs. giving up

The inward strength to withstand the stress to accomplish God's best.

"And let us not lose heart in doing good, for in due time we shall reap if we do not grow weary." *(Galatians 6:9)*

☐   ☐   ☐   **17. Enthusiasm** vs. apathy

Expressing with my spirit the joy of my soul.

"Rejoice always; pray without ceasing; in everything give thanks; for this is God's will for you in Christ Jesus. Do not quench the Spirit." *(1 Thessalonians 5:16-18)*

☐   ☐   ☐   **18. Faith** vs. presumption

Visualizing what God intends to do in a given situation and acting in harmony with it.

"Now faith is the assurance of things hoped for, the conviction of things not seen." *(Hebrews 11:1)*

NW   NS   AM

☐   ☐   ☐   **19. Flexibility** vs. resistance

Not setting my affections on ideas or plans, which could be changed by God or others.

"Set your mind on the things above, not on the things that are on earth." (Colossians 3:2)

☐   ☐   ☐   **20. Forgiveness** vs. rejection

Clearing the record of those who have wronged me, and allowing God to love them through me.

"And be kind to one another, tenderhearted, forgiving each other, just as God in Christ also has forgiven you." (Ephesians 4:32)

☐   ☐   ☐   **21. Generosity** vs. stinginess

Realizing that all I have belongs to God and using it for His purposes.

"Now this I say, he who sows sparingly shall also reap sparingly; and he who sows bountifully shall also reap bountifully." (2 Corinthians 9:6)

☐   ☐   ☐   **22. Gentleness** vs. harshness

Showing personal care and concern in meeting the needs of others.

"But we proved to be gentle among you, as a nursing mother tenderly cares for her own children." (1 Thessalonians 2:7)

NW   NS   AM

☐   ☐   ☐   **23. Gratefulness** vs. un-thankfulness

Making known to God and others in what ways they have benefited my life.

"For who regards you as superior? And what do you have that you did not receive? But if you did receive it, why do you boast as if you had not received it?" (1 Corinthians 4:7)

☐   ☐   ☐   **24. Hospitality** vs. loneliness

Cheerfully sharing food, shelter, and spiritual refreshment with those who God brings into my life.

"Do not neglect to show hospitality to strangers, for by this some have entertained angels without knowing it." (Hebrews 13:2)

☐   ☐   ☐   **25. Humility** vs. pride

Seeing the contrast between God's holiness and my sinfulness.

"But he gives a greater grace. Therefore it says, "God is opposed to the proud, but gives to the humble." (James 4:6)

☐   ☐   ☐   **26. Initiative** vs. unresponsiveness

Recognizing and doing what needs to be done before I am asked to do it.

"Do not be overcome by evil, but overcome evil with good." (Romans 12:21)

NW   NS   AM

☐   ☐   ☐   **27. Joyfulness** vs. self-pity

The result of knowing that God is perfecting His life in others through me.

"A joyful heart makes a cheerful face, but when the heart is sad, the spirit is broken." *(Proverbs 15:13)*

☐   ☐   ☐   **28. Justice** vs. fairness

Personal responsibility to God's unchanging laws.

"He had told you, O man, what is good; and what does the Lord require of you but to do justice, to love kindness, and to walk humbly with your God?" (Micah 6:8)

☐   ☐   ☐   **29. Love** vs. selfishness

Giving to others' basic needs without having personal rewards as my motive.

"And if I give all my possessions to feed the poor, and if I deliver my body to be burned, but do not have love, it profits me nothing." *(1 Corinthians 13:3)*

☐   ☐   ☐   **30. Loyalty** vs. unfaithfulness

Using difficult times to demonstrate my commitment to God and to those whom he has called me to serve.

"Greater love has no one than this, that one lay down his life for his friends." (John 15:13)

NW   NS   AM

☐   ☐   ☐   **31. Meekness** vs. anger

Yielding my personal rights and expectations to God.

"My soul, wait in silence for God only, for my hope is from him." (Psalm 62:5)

☐   ☐   ☐   **32. Obedience** vs. willfulness

Fulfilling instructions so that God and the one I am serving will fully be satisfied.

"We are destroying speculations and every lofty thing raised up against the knowledge of God, and we are taking every thought captive to the obedience of Christ." (2 Corinthians 10:5)

☐   ☐   ☐   **33. Orderliness** vs. disorganization

Arranging my life and surroundings so that God has maximum freedom to achieve His goals through me.

"But let all things be done properly and in an orderly manner." (1 Corinthians 14:40)

☐   ☐   ☐   **34. Patience** vs. restlessness

Accepting a difficult situation from God without giving Him a deadline to remove it.

"And not only this, but we also exult in our tribulations, knowing that tribulation brings about perseverance; and perseverance, proved character; and proven character, hope." (Romans 5:3-4)

NW	NS	AM
☐	☐	☐

35. Persuasiveness vs. contentiousness

Using words which cause the listener's spirit to confirm that he is hearing truth.

"And the Lord's bondservant must not be quarrelsome, but be kind to all, able to teach, patient when wronged." (2 Timothy 2:24)

☐	☐	☐

36. Punctuality vs. tardiness

Showing respect for other people and the limited time that God has given to them.

"There is an appointed time for everything. And there is a time for every event under heaven" (Ecclesiastes 3:1)

☐	☐	☐

37. Resourcefulness vs. wastefulness

Wise use of that which others would normally overlook or discard.

"He who is faithful in a very little thing is faithful also in much; and he who is unrighteous in a very little thing is unrighteous also in much." (Luke 16:10)

☐	☐	☐

38. Responsibility vs. unreliability

Knowing and doing what God and others are expecting from me.

"So then each one of us shall give account of himself to God." (Romans 14:12)

NW   NS   AM

☐   ☐   ☐   **39. Reverence** vs. disrespect

Awareness of how God is working through the people and events in my life to produce the character of Christ in me.

"Do not let your heart envy sinners, but live in the fear of the Lord always." (Proverbs 23:17)

☐   ☐   ☐   **40. Security** vs. anxiety

Structuring my life around what is eternal and cannot be destroyed or taken away.

"Do not work for the food which perished, but for the food which endures to eternal life, which the Son of Man shall give to you, for on Him the Father, even God, has set His seal." (John 6:27)

☐   ☐   ☐   **41. Self-control** vs. self-indulgence

Instant obedience to the initial prompting of God's Spirit.

"Now those who belong to Christ Jesus have crucified the flesh with its passions and desires. If we live by the Spirit, let us also walk by the Spirit." (Galatians 5:24-25)

☐   ☐   ☐   **42. Sensitivity** vs. callousness

Knowing by the prompting of God's Spirit what words and actions will benefit the lives of others.

"Rejoice with those who rejoice, and weep with those who weep." (Romans 12:15)

NW   NS   AM

☐   ☐   ☐   **43. Sincerity** vs. hypocrisy

Eagerness to do what is right with transparent motives.

"Since you have in obedience to the truth purified your souls for a sincere love of the brethren, fervently love one another from the heart." (1 Peter 1:22)

☐   ☐   ☐   **44. Thriftiness** vs. extravagance

Not letting myself or others spend that which is not necessary.

"If therefore you have not been faithful in the use of unrighteous mammon, who will entrust the true riches to you?" (Luke 16:11)

☐   ☐   ☐   **45. Thoroughness** vs. incompleteness

Realizing that each of our tasks will be reviewed and rewarded by God.

"The mind of the prudent acquire knowledge, and the ear of the wise seeks knowledge." (Proverbs 18:15)

☐   ☐   ☐   **46. Tolerance** vs. prejudice

Viewing every person as a valuable individual who God created and loves.

"Make my joy complete by being of the same mind, maintaining the same love, united in spirit, intent on one purpose." (Phillipians 2:2)

NW	NS	AM
☐	☐	☐

47. Truthfulness vs. deception

Earning future trust by accurately reporting facts.

"Therefore, laying aside falsehood, speak truth, each one of you, with his neighbor, for we are members of one another." (Ephesians 4:25)

| ☐ | ☐ | ☐ |

48. Wisdom vs. natural inclinations

Seeing and responding to life situations from God's frame of reference.

"The fear of the Lord is the beginning of wisdom, and the knowledge of the Holy One is understanding." (Proverbs 9:10)

| ☐ | ☐ | ☐ |

49. Virtue vs. impurity

The influence God is having on others through my life, regardless of my past failures.

"Seeing that His power has granted to us everything pertaining to life and Godliness, through the true knowledge of Him who called us by His glory and excellence." (2 Peter 1:3)

*"The Rebuilder's Guide, pages 170-175. Used by permission. Institute in Basic Life Principles. www.iblp.org."

You might be thinking, *Great, now I know what my Kryptonite is, but how do I go about getting rid of it?*

Well, I will tell you the three things I've done that have dramatically reduced the amount I let my Kryptonite control my actions.

1. Admit To Another
2. Pray
3. Trust

The first thing is to openly and honestly admit to someone you trust that you have an issue with these things, and you want that person to hold you accountable by giving you a little nudge when they see you operating with Kryptonite in hand. There is so much power with just admitting that we struggle with something. That in itself helps, but the accountability of another knowing to keep you on your toes when they see it in action will reduce it radically.

Second, pray. I pray this exact prayer almost daily, because pride is really my biggest Kryptonite:

"God, take this **pride** *away from me that keeps me from becoming the Hero you have designed me to be."*

You can insert anything into where I have pride emphasized, and let God take it away from you. It works, I promise.

And finally, the third thing is to just trust. Trust me when I say to you that going through the gutting process will give you vision into why you struggle with certain things, and how to overcome them. And that vision of "WHY" brings a clarity that leads to "HOW."

Our individual Kryptonite is easy to identify, even if we aren't looking for it. There is always some little energy within ourselves that sparks when we see, hear, or read something that reminds us of what we know, deep in our soul, that we need to work on. It's almost as if God put this little alarm clock inside of us to keep us on our toes.

Next Steps

Now that you've gone through this process and taken an honest look at where you think you are in relation to these 49 qualities, I want you to take it two steps further.

1. I want you to go here: www.timmitchum.com/thb/49qualities, and print out the list and give it to someone who knows you to fill out as they see you. This could be your wife, girlfriend, mentor, father, mother, or anyone who would know you well enough to do it honestly. This may sound a little scary, but it will give you great insight into what others see that maybe you don't.

2. I would plan on doing this exercise once a year, to see how you improve. We will never get to perfect; being human, that isn't possible, but we can continually strive to close the gap on where we are to where we want to be.

Step 6:
SUBMITTING TO YOUR MORAL COMPASS

"Succeeding or getting to the top at all costs
is by definition an immoral goal." Jon M. Huntsman

When I started writing this chapter, the original title was "Fixing Your Moral Compass," but soon after I started, I realized, it doesn't need to be fixed. It's actually never been broken. What we need to do is become someone who submits to it without apprehension.

Life becomes very simple when you finally decide to submit to your moral compass on what is right, and eliminate actions that tend to contradict what it is telling you. It doesn't mean life becomes easy; far from it, but it definitely becomes less confusing, which makes it much simpler.

I spent a lot of my life with a moral compass that I manipulated to give me the direction that made the most sense to my selfish nature, at the expense of what was morally right. In other words, I didn't submit to its direction. But at some point, if you truly want to live and die as a Hero, you have to commit to submitting to the moral compass, which has been with you since birth. We have to end the habit of justification. We have to Right the Ship, so that we can sail smoothly, even in the roughest of waters.

This process is actually very freeing.

Chances are there is somebody who comes to your mind when you think about submitting to a moral compass. The type of person who you know will do the right thing, regardless of the consequences. This person is actually in a lot less sticky situations to have to prove themselves, because their submission to their moral compass keeps them out of them in the first place. But you respect this person, because they have this power that is so hard to find in our world today.

One person who comes to mind to me is Jon M. Huntsman. Even if you don't know who Mr. Huntsman is, I guarantee he has had an effect on your life at some point. Jon Huntsman is the founder of Huntsman Chemical, which at one point was a 12 billion dollar privately-held company that produced, among other things, the plastic egg carton, the Big Mac container, and plastic silverware. He also is the author of the book *Winners Never Cheat*, and in it outlines the way he built this massively successful business and life by focusing on doing the right thing in every situation. There is a story from his book that really stood out to me, and I would like to share it with you here so you can see firsthand what it's like to live successfully by submitting to your moral compass regardless of consequences.

In his words:

"Bribes and scams may produce temporary advantages, but the practice carries an enormous price tag. It cheapens the way business is done, temporarily enriches a few corrupt individuals, and makes a mockery of the rules of play.

In the 1980s, Huntsman Chemical opened a plant in Thailand. Mitsubishi was a partner in this joint venture, which we called HMT. With about $30 million invested, HMT announced the construction of a second site. I had a working relationship with the country's minister of finance, who never missed an opportunity to suggest it could be closer.

I went to his home for dinner one evening, where he showed me 19 new Cadillacs parked in his garage, which he described as "gifts" from foreign companies. I explained that the Huntsman Company didn't engage in that sort of thing, a fact he smilingly acknowledged.

Several months later, I received a call from the Mitsubishi executive in Tokyo responsible for Thailand operations. He stated HMT had to pay various government officials kickbacks annually to do business and that our share of this joint obligation was $250,000 for that year.

I said we had no intention of paying even five cents toward what was nothing more than extortion. He told me every company in Thailand paid these "fees" in order to be guaranteed access to the industrial sites. As it turned out, and without our knowledge, Mitsubishi had been paying our share up to this point, as the cost of doing business, but had decided it was time Huntsman Chemical carried its own baggage.

The next day, I informed Mitsubishi we were selling our interest. After failing to talk me out of it, Mitsubishi paid us a discounted price for our interest in HMT. We lost about $3 million, short term. Long haul, it was blessing in disguise. When the Asian economic crisis came, several years down the road, the entire industry went under.

In America and Western Europe, we proclaim high standards when it comes to such things as paying bribes, but we don't always practice what we preach. Ethical decisions can be cumbersome and unprofitable in the near term, but after our refusal to pay "fees" in Thailand became known, we never had a problem over bribes again in that part of the world. The word got out: Huntsman just says no. And so do many other companies.

Once you compromise your values by agreeing to bribes or payoffs, it is difficult ever to reestablish your reputation or credibility. Therefore, carefully choose your partners, be they individuals, companies, or nations."

There are three things in this story that really stand out to me, that can be applied to any situation in life.

When Mr. Hunstman first met for dinner with the minister of finance, it was obvious by his comments that he expected gifts of some sort from any foreign company wanting to do business there. Mr. Huntsman immediately responded to those comments with comments of his own that showed his moral compass would not be allowing that to happen. He immediately recognized and addressed the situation that was threatening his moral compass. *Preventative Action.*

When confronted with the information that his partners at Mitsubishi were paying these kickbacks without his knowledge, now expecting Mr. Huntsman to pick up his portion as a part of doing business, he did not hesitate with the appropriate response. The very next day he said they would no longer be doing business over there, and they would take a loss to get out of the situation that was not congruent with his moral compass. He immediately recognized and addressed the situation that was threatening his moral compass. *Definitive Action.*

Mr. Huntsman's decision was eventually confirmed with the knowledge that getting out of the deal he was invested in and losing money short-term was actually a net long-term gain. *Blessing.*

When we start to submit to our moral compass, there is a pattern that will continue to reveal itself which, over time, will encourage this submission to become a habit. This pattern is outlined in the story of Mr. Huntsman. Initially, there is something that triggers our compass to fire a warning shot of sorts across the bow of our mental ship. At this point we either take preventative action to try to nip the issue in the bud, before it becomes a situation, or we don't.

Hopefully, we stop it quickly, but in the case that our preventative action doesn't detour it, we have to take quick, strategic, and massive action to solve it.

When I first read this story, I couldn't believe he literally cut ties the next day, and chose to lose three million dollars to get out of the situation. Three million might not be that much to a billionaire, but I'm sure the projected profits he was walking away from at the time would have kept most people from pulling out. He didn't, and in the end he was blessed, which is what I've found to be the typical return on your investment when you get into the habit of submitting to your moral compass. Keep this formula in mind at all times when it comes to dealing with those situations that come up in life that will test our ability to submit to our moral compass.

Preventative Action + Definitive Action = Blessing

Step 7:

SERVING PLAN

"Learn the word No, so you can love the word Yes." Tim Mitchum

I have a motto. Right or wrong, it is my motto, and has served me well over the years, or at least the last five years. *Don't serve if you can't do it joyfully, but don't make excuses if you can, and your favorite TV show is the only thing standing in the way.* That's the rough version, and I'm sure there's a more eloquent version out there somewhere, but that will have to do, for now. Let me explain a little better.

I am a pew baby. What I mean by that is that I've been going to church since the day I was born, with a few years of rebellion scattered throughout. I've had the opportunity to lead worship at a few churches, for about 10 years, and have really gotten the behind-the scenes-view of what goes on. The main thing I've noticed is that these churches are made up of people who are human, who do all the same great and stupid things that we humans do every day. They are no different, and there are no "super" Christians who make up a church staff, at least that I have run across. There seems to be this black hole of church volunteering which, if you fall into it, you can't get out, and you're committed to saying yes to anything related to church. I'm sure there are churches out there that unnecessarily pressure its members to the extreme, but I've found that most of the pressure is put on us by ourselves.

Even though a lot of us typically think of serving as within the Church, there are a lot of other serving or volunteering opportunities outside of the church that you may be involved with, now or in the past. Regardless of what type of opportunity it is, I've noticed three types of servants who are pretty common to any situation. You will most likely identify with one of these prior to us defining it.

1. The Identity Servant

2. The Resentful Servant

3. The Joyful Servant

Let's look at the Identity Servant, and what I mean by that. This is the easiest of all servants to identify, unless you fall into this category. If that is the case, you probably can't think of this person, which means it is most likely you. It was me for at least five years of my worship leading.

If being an identity servant was similar to the flu, some common symptoms that easily identify this person follow:

1. They have been doing the exact same serving function longer than most, and asking them to step down from this function would take committees of people to figure out how to handle the collateral damage and emotional fallout it most likely will cause.

2. They tend to criticize first, blame second, and verbally or emotionally abuse third.

3. A word that follows them is Diva or Divo, I am not even sure if Divo is a word, but regardless of gender, it is obviously all about them. Period.

On the other hand, the second kind of servant I've noticed is what I call the Resentful servant. Here are some common ways to identify this person.

1. They have a really hard time saying no.

2. They commit to something, but tend to be sporadic in their participation. They may have the habit of showing up late, forgetting meetings and events, or leaving early.

3. Inside, they feel burnt out, stretched to the limit, and resentful to the people who continue to ask them to do things, but also to themselves for not knowing how to say no.

And finally we come to the last type of servant, who I call the Joyful servant. This is the one we will focus on becoming. Here are some things you might notice about the joyful servant.

1. They are as comfortable saying the word "no" as they are the word "yes."

2. Very reliable. They are usually early and stay late.

3. They are energized by the experience, and energize those around them.

Did you see yourself identifying with any of those servant personalities? Chances are you did, and I hope you fell into the Joyful Servant category, but from my experience there is a good chance that you didn't. If serving hasn't been a big part of your life up to this point, then don't worry about fitting yourself into one of these categories. You will have a huge advantage as you begin to create this piece of your life so that you do it joyfully, and not any other way.

I was definitely the Identity Servant for a few years of my life. I was asked to do some worship leading at my church. Since I could barely sing, barely play the guitar, and barely keep a rhythm, it meant that I had all the skills needed to lead worship at a church in need of worship leaders!

But for some reason I was really drawn to wanting to do it. I had played in the bars for a lot of years, all the good old sing-along songs to my adoring fans, who could barely stand up. I had taken a step back from that, for the most part, because I was tired of playing to a crowd of drunks who just wanted to sing *Brown Eyed Girl* until two in the morning. It wasn't very fulfilling, after a while, but it did provide me a moment of stardom that I was drawn to. So, when I was asked to lead worship, what came out of my mouth was, "I would love to do this to serve God and use what skill I had to do some of his work." What my heart was really saying was, "This is my chance to shine and get the rock star feeling again."

Because I wasn't aware at the time that my heart wasn't in the right place, spiritually, and I was leading worship primarily to fulfill a need in me, I didn't notice some of my actions that were tell-tale signs of an Identity Servant. I was constantly complaining, if not outwardly, inwardly, about song selection, sound quality, attitudes of the worship team, other leaders, and on and on. It got to the point where my attitude was that these people at this church had no idea how to do worship, and if they would do what I say, the worship would be much better.

You could call me a Divo, in the sense that it was way more about me than about the church or serving God. At this point in my life, I really didn't want to quit, even though there was no joy in it for me, because it had kind of become my spiritual identity. I really liked the compliments, and fed off of the ego trip it gave me to hear someone say how much they liked it when I led worship. Eventually, I realized that my heart was not in the right place if all I did was complain about how things were done and about the people doing them, so I quit leading. It turned out to be a good decision. I had fallen into the Identity Servant role, and wasn't really doing anybody any good with the attitude or lack of willingness to submit to the leadership that God had placed in that church.

Fast forward three years, after leaving that church and starting down this Heroes Blueprint Journey, I was finally in the right place to serve joyfully. I knew it, because I was attending my current church and felt like there was an opportunity to offer my skills in any way that I could, without demands on my part. I could play piano, guitar, sing, and lead if they wanted me to, or do nothing if I didn't make the cut. It was really okay either way, because my heart was finally in the place to offer skills to be used for whatever need was there, and not to shine for my own ego. I was placed on multiple teams to play some guitar, a little piano, and just help out where I was needed, and it was fun again. It was joyful to serve. Turns out a year or so after getting on the worship team for this church, I was asked to lead a service in the basement for the small service of about 50 people, and that was just fine with me because it wasn't about me. I made sure that I was upfront about what level of commitment I could make in order to do a great job, and do it joyfully. That was my only "prerequisite," and it has worked out great.

Let's take a look at the Resentful Servant. If you found yourself identifying with this servant personality, chances are you've been told before that you are a "people pleaser." You most likely have a really hard time saying no to someone, especially when it comes to helping others. The thing that's confusing about this servant personality is that sometimes they tend to come off as overly joyful. Like there is nothing in the world that they would rather be doing, but inside they are on the edge of burnout, and the overly joyful or happy attitude is the fake fuel they use to get them through the deal that they are overcommitted to. They haven't learned to say no in order to keep the balance they need to serve joyfully in whatever it is they're doing.

They also tend to be binge servants. They're all in for a long time on lots of different volunteering or serving opportunities, and then crash and disappear for a while, and quit serving all together. They eventually become resentful of people taking advantage of them, but mostly at themselves for not being able to control their own life. The good news about Resentful Servants is that usually their hearts are in the right place, and when they get a handle on balance and time management, they do great things.

So how do we become the Joyful Servant? It took me a lot of years to get to this place, and I want to share with you how I went from Identity Servant to Joyful Servant. I never really landed on Resentful Servant, because I was always way better at saying no than yes. There's a formula I ended up creating and using that gives me balance, and I'm hoping it gives you balance, too.

The first thing that I do is identify the different types of needs or opportunities to volunteer or serve. I put these needs into one of these categories:

1. Skill Needs

2. Passion Needs

3. Short-Term Needs

4. Long-Term Needs

Skill needs are needs that I see that would benefit from the skills I have. For instance, serving on the worship team fits the skills I have as a musician. Even though I'm a completely average musician, there's still a skill need fit there, as long as the church can find uses for my abilities.

Passion needs are needs that align with my passions. A perfect example of this is facilitating the "Quest for Authentic Manhood" course with a group of guys. I absolutely have a passion for continuous learning on how to become a better man, and sharing this information with other guys, and the camaraderie, friendships, and life-changes that you see happen.

Short-term and long-term are fairly self-explanatory. I take all these needs that I see around me and decide whether they are a skill or passion need, as well as a short-term or long-term need. I personally classify short-term as anything less than three months, and long-term as anything from three months to forever. There isn't a perfect science as to why I chose to break short-term and-long term at three months. It just felt right, and has worked out well for me.

This yearly serving plan is something I typically do around the holidays, planning for the next year, and it's never perfect. Things change, life changes, but I always start with a plan. For me, personally, my schedule allows me to JOYFULLY do a certain amount of volunteering and serving. For you, it will be different. I recommend erring on the less than you think you can do side, so you don't get caught up in burnout. I know some people will disagree with me on this, and that's okay, but my goal is for you to become joyful about serving, not someone who is known for the amount that they serve. I want you to be effective, not just a warm body that shows up.

To give you an example, to hopefully help you get an idea of what I am talking about, my serving plan may look like this on any given year.

1. I choose one long-term skill need that I can do effectively, and set the amount of time I'm willing to invest. So, for instance, I committed up front to leading worship six times a year, and I can do it without complaining. Much more than six times, and I will not do it joyfully. I've been there, done that, and will not let myself do it again.

2. I choose one long-term passion need that I can do, that doesn't take up more than one night a week. For me, at this point, that is the Quest for Authentic Manhood course I facilitate, and it goes for 26 weeks at a time.

3. I leave myself open for two short-term passion needs, like being an assistant coach for the YMCA here in my hometown. I usually assist a head coach, as coaching isn't necessarily a skill or passion of mine, but I can give a heck of a high five to encourage the kids. The kids are definitely the passion in this deal, and whether it is an 8-week basketball or 6-week football season, it is worth it.

If you aren't currently serving joyfully, I assure you that you can get there! Becoming a Joyful Servant took me a few years, only because I didn't realize that I was the real problem, and not someone else, but it doesn't have to take you that long. Part of the gutting process will reveal what you need to do in order to humble yourself, as in my case, or to give yourself the permission and the courage to say no, in order to keep you from becoming resentful. Once we get our hearts in the right place, the serving and volunteering becomes extremely fulfilling.

Go through this process and find out what works best for you. Everybody is different, everybody has different time constraints, but we all have the deep down desire to serve. Sometimes we just need a little priming on the old pump to get us moving. This is your priming. Now get pumping!

Quick Skills and Passions Assessment

Go ahead and take a few minutes to write down skills and passions you have that can be used in various serving situations. Don't get caught up in the "uniqueness" or lack thereof with any skills. This exercise is just to get you thinking about what they are, so that opportunities will be easier to identify. After doing that, I want you to do the same thing with your passions.

Skills I possess that can be used to serve at some point:

_____

_____

_____

_____

_____

_____

Passions I have:

_____

_____

_____

_____

_____

_____

Step 8:

MENTORING PLAN

"Life's too hard to figure it out on your own." Author Unknown

Before I started going through this Heroes Blueprint, I thought of mentoring as something you only did in the business setting. One of the definitions of "mentor" is *"to serve as a trusted counselor or teacher, especially in occupational settings."* There was even an article in a local paper just yesterday, as I write this, headlined, "The Importance of Mentors." I opened the paper to read it, but to my disappointment it was all about getting ahead in business.

Don't get me wrong, mentors in business are great, and I've had a few who helped me tremendously to make certain connections and better decisions to increase my income and get ahead in business.

But what we're talking about here is much different. You see, I know lots of people who are "successful" in business, and absolute train wrecks in life. They had great business mentors, and it definitely paid off with wealth of the monetary kind, but what about their personal lives? How much did they sacrifice by having a singular focus on money?

You see, the Transformational Hero sees money not as an identity, but as a way to better fulfill their destiny to transform the lives of those around them. The first thing that we have to understand is there is a distinct difference between a business mentor and one who is focused on life skills. The Hero recognizes this distinction, and has a mentoring plan in place for both, but for our purposes we're going to talk about mentoring for life, and not business.

My first experience on the receiving end of a mentoring relationship was through the Big Brothers & Big Sisters program when I was 10 years old. Since I had grown up without a father in the house, my mom signed me up for the program, and one cold snowy Iowa night I saw this beat-up station wagon pull into the driveway. I was sitting on the couch in the living room, watching through the frosted window, thinking, "I wonder what this guy is going to be like?" When he got out of the car, he trudged through the snow in his 3-piece suit, wearing rubbers over his wingtip shoes to make it up to the door. When he came inside, I met Kirt for the first time.

Kirt and I are I friends to this day, 27 years later. He came into my life at a pivotal time, and breathed life into me when I needed it most. I knew for the first time that someone was watching, and it felt good.

If you're thinking that you don't have what it takes to be a mentor, then let me set your mind at ease. You do.

In Robert Lewis's "Quest for Authentic Manhood" course, he talks about mentors being specialists. They are really there to help you get from point A to B at a certain place in your life. A mentor is one who supports, as opposed to competes. They are one who is primarily a cheerleader, not a critic. They are one who seeks to encourage the development of your gifts, while seeking to protect you from costly mistakes. They admire and delight in you, because they instinctively recognize your value and untapped potential. They are not necessarily a close friend, but are a close confidant, or a safe person.

He continues to talk about what the mentor brings to the table as the following:

1. Wisdom through experience

2. Warnings

3. A belief in you

4. Cheers for your achievement

5. In some instances…a proven hero

You see, you have all of those things. I guarantee it. You have wisdom, because you've been somewhere in life that a younger individual has not. You're able to give warnings based on your mistakes. You can believe in someone else in order to breathe life into them. You can cheer, and eventually become a hero to them. You can transform their life, even if in the smallest of ways, to help them get from point A to point B.

There are lots of books out there that go into very specific types of mentoring, and can almost make you feel overwhelmed. For our purposes, we're going to briefly talk about three mentoring relationships that you should start to implement in your life. Once you start to implement this part of the blueprint, you will start to immediately reap the rewards.

There are three main types of mentoring relationships you need to have in your life.

1. Downward Mentoring

2. Side-by-Side Mentoring

3. Upward Mentoring

We saw a really good example of Downward Mentoring with Kirt investing in me through the Big Brothers & Big Sisters program. Downward Mentoring is when you invest in someone younger to help them get to another place in their life, and then let them go. You strategically let them go in order for them to be able to find another mentor to continue helping them on their journey. Kirt and I are still friends out of choice, because I just flat-out love that guy, and he loves me.

Right now I'm involved with a local YMCA program with inner city youth through sports as my Downward Mentoring piece of my life. I love it. It's amazing to see a kid's chest puff out, his shoulders pull back, and his eyes light up from simply encouraging them, supporting them, cheering for them, and believing in them. Telling a kid you believe in them breathes life into them like you can't imagine. It also breathes life into you.

There are so many opportunities to Downward Mentor that it is mind-blowing. In the back of this book I am going to list numerous programs that you can look into in order to fill this piece of your life.

With Side-by-Side mentoring, we basically come alongside of someone who we have a connection with, to hold each other accountable, celebrate victories, find the lessons in the defeats and encourage each other on the quest to becoming the person we've decided we want to be. I have a couple of Side-by-Side Mentoring relationships with close friends. In order to have a successful Side-by-Side Mentoring relationship, you must have a common bond that usually defines how you're going to live your life. Our common bond is our faith. When we spend an hour every couple of weeks together, we talk about how we're doing in relationship to our faith, what we're struggling with, plans to eliminate obstacles, and just general life stuff. We add value to each other, and wisdom based on our common bond. You challenge each other, celebrate the victories from those challenges, and create strategies on how to overcome the losses.

And the last of the three is Upward Mentoring, in which you find someone older who can help you get to the next level of life that you're reaching for.

In his book, *As Iron Sharpens Iron*, Dr. Howard Hendricks lays out what you need to look for in a good Upward Mentor as the following:

1. They clearly have what you personally need.

2. They choose to cultivate a relationship with you.

3. They are willing to take a chance on you.

4. They are respected by others.

5. They have a network of resources.

6. They are consulted by others.

7. They both talk and listen.

8. They are consistent in their lifestyle.

9. They are able to diagnose your real needs.

10. They are concerned with your interests.

When you find this Upward Mentor, it not only blesses you, but it completely blesses them, just like your Downward Mentoring blesses you. It's really such a cool thing that most people miss out on in life; having a strategic mentoring plan in place that will actually give them life later on. I currently have two Upward Mentors, one who is intentional and strategic, and another who is occasional and not so strategic. They both breathe life into me, and me into them.

I asked my occasional Upward Mentor, one day, what he was going to do when he retires, and he said, "I'm going to travel and spend time mentoring others." You see, he has it figured out, and this mentoring in the later years of his life is actually giving him life. It allows him to teach from his experience, and that gives him significant purpose that closes the loop on his life cycle. I told him one day that I was coaching down at the YMCA, and he put his hand on my shoulder and said, "I am so proud of you." I might as well have been a 10 year old kid who just hit a home run as my chest puffed out, my shoulders pulled back and my eyes lit up. He had just breathed life into me, and I into him.

As for my other upward mentor relationship, it's much more intentional. We have a plan for me to achieve certain things in life, and work that plan. He honors me by being intentional and strategic in helping me meet the goals we set out, and I honor him by doing the work required to make his effort rewarded with results.

I feel very blessed to have mentoring relationships in all three categories, which is my goal for you, as well. I could probably write a whole book on how much these relationships will change your life, but the fact is that you need to experience it for yourself. This is a crucial component to becoming a Transformational Hero. As you go through the steps in this Heroes Blueprint, you will start to understand your history, pain, and talents that will enable you to really enter into the world of another.

So put together your strategy to invest and be invested in by others. Start to seek out what opportunities fit you, and who it is that makes sense for you to ask. Take some training on becoming a mentor. Read the books recommended in the back of this book, so that you can be the best mentor and mentoree that you can. Whatever you do, don't pass over this step, because it may just be the most important part of this process.

Identifying Mentor Opportunities

We've learned about three different types of mentoring relationships that we need to eventually be involved with. Those three were as follows:

1. Downward Mentoring
2. Side-by-Side Mentoring
3. Upward Mentoring

Take a moment to list a few names in each of these categories that might make sense to start developing a mentor relationship.

Downward Mentors (Younger individuals who can benefit from your wisdom and life experience)

_____

_____

_____

_____

_____

_____

_____

Side-by-Side Mentors (Individuals who can challenge you, and who you can challenge through a shared common bond or life perspective)

_____

_____

_____

_____

_____

_____

_____

Upward Mentors (Those who have what YOU need)

_____

_____

_____

_____

_____

_____

_____

_____

Step 9:

LINING UP YOUR DESIGNATED STONE THROWER

"Sometimes the only way you can take a really good look at yourself is through somebody else's eyes." ~From the television show, Scrubs

When I started to write this book and lay out the Heroes Blueprint, this step 9 wasn't included. But after really going through this process and seeing the great rewards of following through, I realized there was a little piece missing, that needed to be addressed.

What exactly is a designated stone thrower? Well, this concept comes straight from the Bible, when Jesus is about to teach to a group of people in John 8. The local Pharisees and leaders brought forth this woman who had committed adultery, which at that time was also called prostitution, to be held accountable for her actions. The law was to stone her to death. Well, the old Pharisees and leaders wanted to trick Jesus and see if he would go against the law that was in place.

They confronted Jesus and said, "Teacher, this woman was caught in the act of adultery. The Law of Moses commanded us to stone such women. Now what do you say?"

Jesus, being the cool cat that he was, bent down and started to draw in the sand, as if these big accusations and these religious leaders weren't really all that important. Every time I read this, I can't help but wonder what he was actually drawing in the sand. I mean, seriously, if I was one of those Pharisees, I think I would have been a little put off by the fact Jesus ignored me and just started drawing in the sand. Some people think Jesus doesn't have a sense of humor. I beg to differ.

When they continued to question him, he stood up straight and said something in a way that only Jesus can, something so simple, yet so powerful, that clearly communicated the truth. Jesus stood up and said, "Let any of you who is without sin be the first to throw the stone at her." And then he stooped back down to the ground and continued writing in the sand.

Well, that pretty much ended the stone throwing, as these men, who were obviously not sinless, who were attempting to condemn this woman, dropped their stones one by one, and walked away. In the end it was just Jesus and this woman. Not a stone was thrown, and he forgave her for her sin.

I tell you this story because it became very apparent to me in my life that if I truly wanted to become the Hero I desired to be, I needed a designated stone thrower.

Sometimes, if you are with the right mentor, they can help you identify sin or habits or patterns in your life that keep you from moving forward and help you move past it. But here's the problem. Most people don't want to start throwing stones, because they're afraid you might just pick up one that hit you in the head and throw it right back. The other problem is that it's hard for us to be really honest, sometimes, with someone we look up to and don't want to disappoint. What I realized is that I needed to find someone that I could be 100% honest with and someone who I, in other words, gave permission to throw stones at me. This person needed to be unbiased and for me. I wanted someone to come from a Biblical perspective. You may be different in the fact that you don't want or need someone with a Biblical perspective, but you definitely need someone who comes from an unbiased perspective.

I committed to lining up this person, but I wasn't exactly sure who this person was supposed to be, or how to get hold of them. I sent out an e-mail to a group of guys whom I trusted from mentoring relationships, telling them I needed to line up this person for my "Life Strategy Team".

I didn't want to say, "Hey, do you know any counselors, because I've got serious problems that I need to talk to someone about." I really didn't feel that way, but I wasn't exactly sure how to word it. I was being proactive, just like you are going to be proactive, because that's what Heroes do.

So, for your information, I've attached the exact email I sent out that led me to the guy who is now my "Designated Stone Thrower."

Subject Line: Need Help

Hey Guys,

I am in the process of building my life "team," as I call it, and I am looking for two things:

1) Overall Life Counselor. Someone I am able to meet with when I can't figure out something on my own and need an unbiased viewpoint to maybe jog something loose.

2) Relationship Counselor. Someone we can go to in order to quickly resolve any relationship issues we are unable to quickly resolve on our own. This person will be part of my conflict resolution strategy, but I am sure we will never have any conflicts that I/we can't resolve...lol... ;)

If you know of anyone that makes sense to recommend for either or both of these, that would be awesome.

Thanks.

So, after pushing send and thinking to myself, "Great, now all these guys are going to think I'm crazy," I got back a name of someone who was recommended that fit both these criteria. So I immediately sent him and e-mail and this that exact e-mail that was sent, for your use if you would like.

Subject Line: "Life Strategy Team" Position Open

I was referred to you by (insert name) who is a very close friend and mentor.

As part of my "life strategy team" that I am always adding to, I am looking to start a relationship with a counselor that I can go to in order to help me discern different life stuff as it comes up.

I understand the value of unbiased knowledge and wisdom outside of my own head, and would like to have someone to meet with as required. I don't have any pressing challenges at the moment, but would like more information about how to benefit from your services.

Cost etc... Thanks for any information. I look forward to talking with you in the near future. You can e-mail me or call anytime.

Sincerely,

Tim Mitchum

With those two emails, I was able to line up and put in place my "Designated Stone Thrower," with whom I meet with as needed. He always gives me his direct, honest perspective on anything that I ask him about, and I give him permission to tell it like he sees it. We don't always agree, and that's okay. I always leave with fresh perspective that I wouldn't have gotten from someone who was worried about their own stuff that I could point out.

The first time we met, he said, laughingly, that he had never had anyone proactively contact him to be a part of a life strategy team. He said, "Anybody who contacts me has a serious issue to deal with, but I've never had anybody contact me for a future preventative type of situation."

I said, "Well, that's because I am going to be a Transformational Hero, and that's what they do."

"Transformational Hero?" he responded. And with that we had our first conversation.

Now you probably noticed in the e-mail that I sent to the guys, I mentioned I was also looking for a relationship counselor. What I was really looking for was a Relationship Conflict Manager, or RCM. As part of the gutting process, I came across a little diagram of how all conflicts go, and I discovered that to truly be effective in life and relationships with your significant other or spouse, you really had to have a plan in place to resolve conflict, so the plan became really simple. When there's an argument, and we cannot seem to find a resolution on our own, we go to see our RCM, and they unbiasly tell us which direction we need to go in order to solve the conflict, and not let the creeping bitterness and creeping separateness sink in as time goes by. The trick is that you both have to agree to yield to the RCM's decision. It cannot be about winning, but has to be about resolution. When we make it about resolution, we grow. When we make it about winning, we always lose.

When you proactively line up these two people, which in my case are the same one, then you will have a huge advantage over others who do not. Those who wait until there is a major issue usually end up with major problems.

The Transformational Hero has the team, strategy, and people in place to keep him light on his feet so he's effective at what's important in life and not held back by burdening issues that haven't been addressed. These two people aren't that much different than a good car mechanic. You can either get towed into the service station or drive in. I think we know which one is more costly.

Step 10:

HERO, INC.

*"The Hero's life is a for-profit business that
produces high-end relationships." Tim Mitchum*

Have you ever thought of running your life like a business? Well, from this point on you are going to start. You see, in order for you to be successful at becoming the Transformational Hero you are going to be, you have to be strategic in your living. This isn't a passive type of life, but one that is very proactive and strategic. You can now think of yourself as the CEO of your very own business, Hero, Inc. For those of you who are business owners or have some background in business, this will be very easy for you to understand.

All businesses produce something. Whether this is a widget, service, information, or any other type of product, the business produces something. And, hopefully, they do it for a profit. They provide something of value to a customer in return for fair compensation for this product. In one of my online businesses, I provide tools to individuals that give them ability to learn how to play the piano with both hands in less than 30 days. In return for this information, they invest a certain amount of money to receive these piano lessons. They receive a lot more value in experience than they invest in dollars.

You can pretty much break any business down into such simple terms, or at least you should be able to, if they know what it is that they actually do well.

When it comes to Hero, Inc., we've already started the process of building our pseudo board of directors with our mentoring plan, along with the addition of the outside consultant, or what I call the "Designated Stone Thrower." We've started lining up people who have a vested interest in our very own Hero, Inc., who we can consult with to make sure the business runs smoothly.

The next things we really need to identify are the different pieces of our business. When I first went through this process, I called it "The Parts of My Life."

The goal here is to identify the different parts of our life that we need to proactively manage, just as if they were pieces of a business, because they are, in essence, and the product we produce are high-end relationships; the best of the best type of relationships with God, significant other, wife, family, friends, co-workers, community, and on and on.

At first, it might seem daunting, but it really isn't. I have a very simple way of running Hero Inc. that I will share with you, which has worked very well for me. We must remember that the goal is to not overwhelm ourselves, but to be strategic in what we do so that we can be effective in life.

When I first started to list the different pieces of Hero, Inc., I came up with, in no particular order, the following:

1. Health

2. Finances/Investments

3. Relationship with Wife

4. Relationship with Family

5. Rings of Friendship

6. Business/Career

7. Serving

8. Mentoring

9. Tithing

10. Mastering my State

11. Goals

12. Faith

13. Hobbies/New FUN Learning

14. Continuous Learning

15. Daily Success Rituals

So that's what I came up with; 15 different pieces of my life that pretty much make up the whole. It's really an eye-opening exercise, because it makes you list, basically, all the pieces that make up your life, and will most likely surprise you one way or the other on how many different pieces there are, or how few. You obviously may have more or less, but this is what it ended up being for me.

After listing these items, I then break each down into smaller pieces, so that I can start to really get a plan together. For instance, health would look something like this:

1. Health

    a. Exercise

   b. Nutrition

   c. Meditation

I would then apply an activity rate to each one of these, so I knew how much I would be focusing on this piece. Health turns into this:

1. Health

   a. Exercise (D)

   b. Nutrition (D)

   c. Meditation (BW)

The (D) stands for Daily, and the (BW) stands for Bi-Weekly. Can it get more simple than that? Probably not, but the fact is that most people don't even write something out that can give them a plan to succeed at in the first place, but you're not going to be that person, because you are following *The Heroes Blueprint* which doesn't allow for slacking.

I go through each of these pieces of my life and break the items down into smaller pieces assigning a daily, weekly, bi-weekly, monthly, bi-monthly, etc. activity rate to it. It's not rocket science, and it isn't perfect, but it gives you a starting point to plan for the week. Because I have these pieces identified, I can sit down on a Sunday night and plan my week, looking to see how to fit in everything I need to do for that week by looking at my Hero, Inc. production schedule.

Now a couple of those on my list may have stood out to you, like "Mastering my State" or the "Rings of Friendship." So let me explain.

I found, time and time again, when I would look at the people I consider successful, that they all had one thing in common. They all were masters of their mental state. They had the ability to weather any storm and come out emotionally unscathed. They also had fearless self-esteem and the courage to accomplish anything. This is truly what I believe made them as successful as they are. I've spent years, and will continue to spend the rest of my life, mastering my mental state through various techniques and exercises.

If you want more information about this process, you should get a book called *Psycho-Cybernetics,* by Maxwell Maltz. This book is an amazing look into how mastering your mental state can change your life.

Now I know you may be thinking that this is an oversimplified way to get a handle on all the pieces of your life. But let me ask you this question, "How difficult do you really want it to be?" There are countless ways to create plans and strategies, and I'm sure mine is not necessarily the best, but it works for me. When I sit down every Sunday night, I know exactly how many things I need to fit into the week to be effective. Do I do it perfectly every time? Uh... No. but I come really close most of the time, and that's better than never all the time. Give yourself some slack, go through the process, and see what you come up with. You might be surprised that with a little planning, you shouldn't be as stressed out as you are. Now that I had to review that list, I notice that I'm slacking on the "Hobbies/New FUN Learning" part of my life. Maybe it's time to head down to the hobby store and find something fun to spend money on, and then wreck. Anyway, you get the drift.

As far as "Rings of Friendship" goes, I'm going to share with you in the next chapter this little thing I developed that literally changed my life and lots of lives around me.

THE RINGS OF FRIENDSHIP

"Just beyond boobs, beer, and balls lies a true Manship." Tim Mitchum

I'm assuming that the majority of you reading this are adult males. With that in mind, I want to ask you a question. How many real man friends do you have? Or, what I coined the term, "Manships." How many real "Manships" do you have that yield conversations that have some depth to them and are not just about boobs, beer, or balls. By balls, I mean sports, in case you were wondering. So how many is it?

Well, if you're like the average American male, it is somewhere around .7 friends each. Can you believe that? .7? That's not even whole person. I can picture two guys sitting at the bar, with one of them missing 30% of their body. And that isn't really even friends of depth, but just what they would call a friend. Most likely someone they would grab a beer with, watch a game, or go to some sporting event together.

As Henry David Thoreau said, *"The mass of men lead lives of quiet desperation."* Do you relate to this quote when you read it? If you do, then you are among the majority, and we're going to change that.

I feel like I've been pretty lucky and blessed to have some really great Manships. But when I heard our Pastor talking about how lonely the American male is, I decided I needed to be more strategic about my relationships with the guys around me. I needed to come up with a plan that would help me get to know these guys better, and develop a system that I could implement to always keep the funnel of new Manships flowing. I know that this may sound a little weird, and there is a good chance it's not normal, but that's the great part about it. I've developed some of the most awesome Manships by being proactive and planning for this piece of Hero, Inc. every week.

Let me explain how the Rings of Friendship works.

The Rings of Friendship is a very simple concept that's designed to identify friendships that I currently have or would be interested in pursuing, and labeling them into one of four categories. I call each category a ring. Let's look at each ring individually, and I'll explain what's involved in each one.

The Distant Ring (Situational)

Who: This ring is made up of individuals who I have had a conversation with at some point that leads me to believe we may have something in common that could lead to a friendship. They're not someone that I typically would ever call on the phone or meet up with, but definitely think that there is something about them that could lead to a better friendship in the future.

A great example of this is when I went ice fishing last winter. I'm not an ice fisherman, but I went because an Inner Circle friend invited me, and I wanted to have a new experience. Not being a seasoned ice fisherman, I didn't have the proper gear, and, when you're in the heart of the Iowa winter, it gets bone-chillingly cold. After drilling what seemed like 1,000 holes to try and find the fish, we settled in to our little tent with the portable heater that was kicking out enough heat to maybe warm a pop can. Needless to say, I was cold. Real cold.

About six hours went by, and I had consumed approximately six Mountain Dews, two bags of chips, a gas station cheeseburger, and some beef jerky, and had caught zero fish. I guess we didn't pick the right hole. Anyway, it was fun despite the lack of fish, just for the conversation with my inner ring buddy. On the way home, we stopped for dinner, as if I needed any more calories, and he invited another buddy of his who was out there to join us. Sitting there, I realized that this friend of his was a really high-quality guy. We aligned on a lot of things, and I knew that he was definitely a candidate for the Distant Ring, so I put him in it.

Let me now explain something about the Distant Ring. The people in this Ring don't know they're in it. They don't know that I hope to move them up at some point, and become better friends. But I do, and they will eventually know.

Ring Activity: Every ring has a plan to it, and, like all my plans, they are very easy to follow and implement. I contact or make sure we run into each other once every six months. Pretty easy, huh? No high pressure; just making sure I keep in contact with them and remind them that I still exist. For instance, with the ice fishing guy, I sent him a message when it got warmer, about five months later and said we should do a little warm weather fishing, which we will.

The next ring is called the Outer Ring. Let's take a look.

The Outer Ring (Activity-Based)

Who: This is an interesting ring, because it is filled with relationships that are probably as deep as most of the typical American male's relationships. When I look at the list, what stands out is that they're really all activity-based relationships. We tend to spend time together because of an event or an activity. The conversations are almost always based on the current event or activity that we're doing. For instance, if I am at a sporting deal, then we're talking sports; if I'm riding Harleys with them in a group, then we're talking about motorcycles; and so on. If it's a full moon, there's a chance someone will bring up a wife or child, but that's very rare. It's all about the activity or event. We don't have any depth, but we have spent a significant amount of time together. When I look at my current list of Outer Ring relationships, I notice that it's all activity-based. It seems like we're always catching up, but not really ever going anywhere.

Ring Activity: I'm pretty much in contact with these guys once a month. If there isn't an event or something, I'll send them an e-mail or pick up the phone and call. My goal is to get them when the time is right to talk about something a little deeper than boobs, beer, and balls. It has to be the right timing, though. One strategy I use with these guys is to start talking about something related to a class I'm facilitating, like "Quest for Authentic Manhood," and let them ask me about that. When they do, I usually get them talking about their father and what their relationship was like, and BAM, they're talking about something they never imagined with another guy, and the walls of protection we hold up start to crumble, just a little bit. If I get them to open up enough to show any real emotions, they're going to move up to the next ring very quickly. I'm only half joking about that, but what happens is that they start to think outside the normal conversations they're used to having. It always starts with me talking about something odd that makes them ask a question that gives me an opening. There's a formula, and it works.

The Inner Ring (Relational)

If the Outer Ring is a kiddie pool, meaning not very deep, then the Inner Ring is more like an Olympic sized swimming pool with a high-dive board.

I remember going to this local neighborhood pool growing up. This was back in the days where kids were allowed to go outside and play without dressing up like storm troopers from Star Wars to make sure they didn't have the opportunity to get a raspberry on their knees or elbows. Some of my great childhood memories of risk and adventure include a memory of stitches somewhere on my body. Today, it's hard to find one of those diving boards that created so much excitement for me, growing up.

Something about walking out to the edge of that high dive and looking down the 10 feet or, what felt like 50 feet, to the water below was exciting and scary at the same time, but what we knew for sure was that the scariest part was jumping. There really wasn't any doubt that we'd be safe, and the water would keep us from getting hurt. All we had to do was jump. The water was deep enough to keep us from hitting the bottom. It was scary, but safe.

Well, that's somewhat like the relationship I have with the Inner Rings guys, so let's talk about what this relationship looks like, and who is in it.

Who: The Inner Ring is made up of guys who at some point have talked about real life stuff, continue to on a regular basis, and not just talk about it in passing. I've listed below the four main conversation categories that are common within the Inner Ring relationship.

1. Dreams

2. Fears or Current Challenges

3. Failures

4. And Successes

As men, we can sometimes try to get a handle on, or deal with, life stuff by basically bottling it up and trying to figure it out on our own, in order to not show any weakness. We're way more inclined to skip over anything deep in order to not really go there. But the fact is that we're all the same, and we all have dreams, fears, failures, and successes. It's easy to talk about the successes, but talking about our fears and failures isn't necessarily what flows from our mouths, especially to another guy.

I can still remember the monumental moment that I first said out loud to another friend that I'd completely failed at something. There was no justification, no rationalization, no blame, and no excuses, but just a flat-out admission that my effort in this thing wasn't good enough, and I failed. It was excruciating for me to admit that to another guy. At that point in my life, a failure in anything, no matter how big or small, was absorbed as an identity, as opposed to an outcome of action or inaction. I've since learned to redefine my definition of success so that I never fail at anything, no matter how big or small, as long as the result is from a 100 percent action-oriented, integrity-driven effort that returns a lesson to be learned.

Point being, within this group of relationships, we talk about real stuff. One thing that I really started to notice about this Ring is that there's a lot of encouragement that goes on. When you talk about real-life stuff, there's a deep-down sense to somehow want to help the other person in any way you can, and that seems to manifest itself through terms of encouragement.

Now don't get me wrong, this group still talks about sports and other guy stuff, but it's nothing to have the conversation go from the NCAA championship game to the struggle they're having at home, and wanting some help discerning how to best handle it.

Ring Activity: I've set a goal to contact these guys, or spend time with the guys in the Inner Circle, at least once a week. This could be a phone call, e-mail, lunch, text message, etc. I usually have lunch or dinner with these guys at least once a month. I never really thought about that until now, as I write this, but I think it's interesting that lunches and dinners really only come into play when you get to this Inner Ring. There's just something about sitting down over a meal and sharing life, I guess.

Now let's take a look at the center of the Rings of Friendship, or what I call the Core Ring where the Core relationships hang out. This is the bullseye of the whole Rings of Friendship deal, and it's open to all but only privy to a few.

The Core Ring (Soul Level)

I have a buddy who is a general surgeon here in Des Moines, Iowa, at Mercy Medical Center, and for a while he lived with me while he was going through his surgical residency. This was back in 2002-2005, and at that point there weren't many rules restricting the amount of hours that a resident could work. It was a brutal schedule he had to go through for years, sometimes leaving at 4:30 AM and not returning for days, and immediately doing it again. There didn't seem to be a real distinction between a weekend and a weekday. I've never seen a person work as hard as he did for that many years straight. For fun, I used to read his medical literature and ask him to test me on how I did with the diagnosis. Needless to say, he humored me, and we had a lot of fun. I still think I could have passed some of those oral boards with just a little more reading, but he might disagree.

One of the really interesting things about him living there was that I got to hear about a lot of the surgeries he did, and all the details on what went right, what went wrong, and how they solved the problem. Pretty amazing to have the curtain peeled back, to some extent, on what goes on behind the surgical drapes. One thing he said that has never left me happened when he was describing a certain surgery he was doing, which involved some very skillful handy-work to avoid creating serious damage that might be unrecoverable. With scalpel in hand, as he was about to cut even deeper into the surgical area they were working on, his senior surgeon leaned over and whispered into his ear, "Be careful; down there is where the soul lives." Can you imagine someone saying that to you as you are about to take a scalpel and cut inside of another person's body? Well, it's no big deal for my surgeon buddy to be comfortable at the soul level in his work any more because of his experience, but the first time his mentor had whispered that into his ear, he definitely took a deep breath.

If the Outer Ring was like a kiddie pool, and the Inner Ring relationship was similar to an Olympic sized swimming pool with a high dive board, then the Core Ring Relationship is like cliff diving into the ocean. You go all in, and you aren't necessarily 100 percent sure you're going to come out unscathed.

When you start doing life at the soul level, there's a vulnerability that most guys are not comfortable with, but are in desperate need of to become the Transformational Hero we're designed to be.

The soul level is where life is, *real life*, the good life. In the Core Relationship, you go to battle for each other to cultivate this divine part of yourselves that leads to your best lives. You challenge, encourage, hold accountable, and provide tools for each other with one goal in mind; to live a soul (spirit)-driven life, and leave the ego-driven life behind. When you start to see the rewards of this change in you, you will never be the same. There's a peace and serenity that comes from living through a soul perspective that cannot be explained in words. Is it possible to ever completely get rid of the ego-driven side of us that leads to excuses, blame, justification, rationalization, and victimization? As long as we're human, I doubt it, but we can always get closer, and that's what the Hero strives for.

Who: There is an unbelievable reward to look back at my Rings of Friendship plan and see a guy who went from the Distant Ring to eventually end up being in the Core Ring. For all the other Rings, I have a "move up" plan that we've looked at, but with the Core Ring I don't really have any control over that. I was trying to figure out how a relationship goes from the Inner Ring to the Core Ring, and I couldn't pinpoint what I did to make that happen. The truth is, I don't think it has anything to do with me. I truly believe that God moves them up in his time, which would make sense, considering we deal at the soul level within the Core, and that my friend is all about God, the divine, or whatever higher power you subscribe to. Bottom line is, it's way bigger than us.

One thing that I do notice about my Core relationships is that we were all involved in a Bible study, worship team, or some other spiritually focused study at some point.

The conversations in the Core Ring are not necessarily a whole lot different than what you find in Inner Ring; it's just they go to the soul level. You still talk about dreams, fears, challenges, failures, and successes, but you deal with them from a soul (spirit) perspective.

Another thing I notice about the Core Relationships is that we've shown a level of affection that some guys never experience from another man in their lives. We tend to hug, as opposed to shake hands, and it's nothing for us to say verbally to each other's faces that we love each other. You may or may not be surprised at how many men I talk to who never even got a hug from their fathers, let alone a verbal, "I love you." Some of that may be a stretch for you, and that's okay, You may be more comfortable with a Budweiser type of, "I love you, man!" but once you start to deal with life on the soul level, you don't get caught up in the semantics of what the world thinks.

Ring Activity: When you get to the Core level with someone, it kind of just works itself out. The difference is that with the Inner Ring you're sharing life together, and with the Core you're more doing life together, so there is always something to talk about, or a reason to get together.

I see my Core guys once every couple of weeks, through coffee, lunches, dinners, just hanging out with the families, Bible studies, talking on the phone, etc. There isn't any type of pressure, and I don't really have a plan for this group. Must be another God thing; his schedule always works better than mine, anyway.

As we come to the end of this chapter you may be thinking that this whole Rings of Friendship thing is...well...cheesy, or not really your deal. I don't blame ya. I mean, seriously, who would actually label a relationship with another guy as a "Manship?" Must be crazy.

Well, the reason I decided share this little strategy with you is because I have been completely shocked and absolutely overwhelmed by how effective this has been. And the truth is, when you start to break out the pieces of your life to start and manage your own Hero, Inc., you can find books, experts, and clear paths to help you with your different pieces, like finances, marriage, raising children, career, jobs, business, investing, family, and so forth. But what there isn't, that I know of, is information on how to implement a system to cultivate relationships with other guys, probably because no guy would buy it, but they all would be blessed by it.

It becomes a really fun deal, because what I haven't told you is that all my Manship prospects, besides the Distant Ring ones, know that they are now in my "Rings of Friendship," but I don't tell them what Ring they are in unless they make it to the Core. If they are a Core friend, they already know it. A lot of them, knowing about the Rings, ask each other, "What ring are you in, in Mitchum's Circle of Friends deal?" I all of a sudden start getting phone calls from guys who say they just wanted to touch base and make sure they don't slip out of the current ring. They also ask what it takes to move up to the next ring, how many rings are there, and what do I have to do to not slip down? It creates a kind of camaraderie that's interesting, to say the least.

I hand out a MIF award every year. This is the Most Improved Friend award, and I actually, believe it or not, get phone calls on who's leading, and bribes with golf outings, motorcycle trips, all of which I'm clear in saying, bribes have no bearing. At least the bribes that I've gotten so far.

If you think you don't need very many friends, and it's not important for you to have some kind of a plan like this, I don't blame ya. But let me share with you a phone call I got from an Inner Ring friend that may make you change your mind. It was actually the moment that I knew the power of the Rings of Friendship model. A good buddy of mine, who'd moved from the Distant to the Outer all the way up to the Inner Ring, called me one day just to tell me how much our friendship has meant to him. He went on to say that it's one of the closest friendships he has ever had with another guy, and that it meant the world to him. He went on to say that he didn't really need his own Rings of Friendship, because he didn't really need that many friends. Just a couple of close ones and that would be enough. I said, "Well, aren't you glad that I didn't feel the same way?" In that moment, he understood for himself the power this simple little plan to create true Manships that go way beyond boobs, beer and balls had in his own life.

The fact is that the only thing in this world that has any true value are relationships; relationships with our God, spouse, kids, family, friends, and community. Maybe it's time for you to implement this simple little plan to start cultivating a few Manships? Or you could go back to talking about boobs, beer, and balls. Your choice.

Your Rings Of Friendship

Now you have the opportunity to create your own "Rings of Friendship" so you can start being more strategic in those relationships. The first thing you're going to want to do is review what type of person goes into what ring. Remember, you can change this any way you want, but I wanted to at least give you a starting point to help you in the beginning of creating your own. The Rings, as I have laid them out, with the type of activity are listed below:

Distant Ring (Situational Relationships)

- Who: This ring is made up of individuals who at some point I have had a conversation with that leads me to believe we may have something in common that could lead to a friendship.

Outer Ring (Activity-Based Relationships)

- Who: Someone who I spend time with because of a mutual activity or event that consistently brings us together. Example; motorcycle group that rides together, tailgating at football games, kids sporting events. You get the picture. All the conversation is based around the event or activity you're currently doing.

Inner Ring (Relational)

- Who: Someone who you continue to talk about real life stuff on a regular basis. For example, 1)Dreams, 2)Fears/or Current Challenges, 3)Failures, 4)Successes. Someone who you give or get encouragement from.

Core Ring (Soul Level)

- Who: Someone who you share all of the Inner Rings things with, but at a soul or spirit level. Even if you aren't sure what that means to you yet, you just know that your relationship with this person is a deep as you've ever had.

Now, using this information, start to fill out your own Rings of Friendship. Don't worry about how many or few that you have in each one. The quantity is unimportant; it's the quality, in the end, that will change your life and the life of the friend.

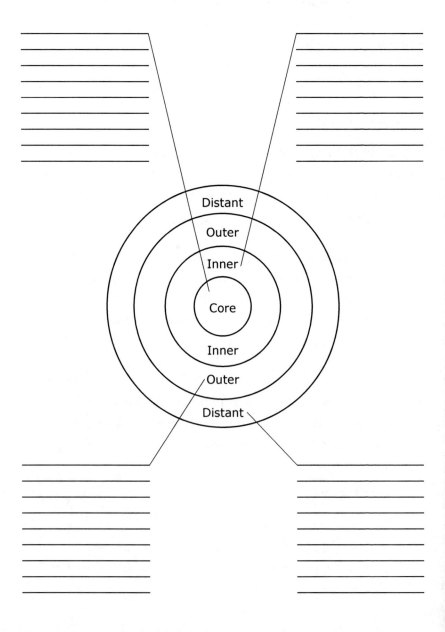

Made To Be A Hero

*"It's okay to think about what you want to do,
until it's time to start doing what you were meant to do."*
From the Disney Movie, "The Rookie"

You were designed, created, and made to be a Hero. You were meant from the very beginning to live a life that transforms the lives of those around you, transforming yours in the process.

There's really no way around this, and we eventually discover this truth whether we want to or not. I was lucky enough to discover this early in life, and not on my deathbed, when I went to confront my Bio Dad. I realized in that moment that he'd missed it. He'd missed real life, he'd missed real love, he'd missed real manhood, and had missed the opportunity to be a Hero. He has missed life for most of his life, and I knew in that moment that I would do whatever was in my power so that it did not happen to me or you.

No matter where you are at in this moment, you can change it. There was a time when I thought I was a lost cause. I lived so selfishly that I couldn't even imagine what it would be like to live out the

Heroes Blueprint. My life was totally self-serving, and because of that it was empty. I was one of the guys who was leading a life of quiet desperation, confused, frustrated, and very alone regardless of how many people were around me. My life could have been defined as "getting through the moment," as opposed to now, which would be "investing in the moment."

I was missing it, and I felt it. I just didn't know what that feeling was, or where it came from.

Are you familiar with that feeling? The feeling that crawls out of your gut and whispers into your ear, "There has to be something more." I promise you there is.

This Heroes Blueprint gives you the step-by-step process that will lead you to the path, and eventually mastery, of becoming the Transformational Hero you are meant to be. It has changed my life, many others lives, and it can and will change your life. All you have to do is be willing to MAN UP and go through the steps. As you do this, keep in mind that becoming a Transformational Hero has nothing to do with feelings, it has everything to do with courage and choice. In other words, we do the right thing, regardless of how it makes us feel, because we've committed to being courageous in doing so. And, eventually, we don't have to think twice.

I think George Bernard Shaw said it very well when he wrote, "This is the true joy of life: being used up for a purpose recognized by yourself as a mighty one; being a force of nature instead of a feverish, selfish, little clot of ailments and grievances, complaining that the world will not devote itself to making you happy."

You will start to see the world differently as you go down this path. You will begin to rise above the fray. You will no longer be a victim of circumstance; you will be a victor over circumstance. You will truly feel like a force of nature in this world as you see the transformation of your life and the lives of others around you, as you put yourself in a position to be invested in, and as you invest in others.

In his course, The *Quest for Authentic Manhood*, Robert Lewis comes up with a definition for what it means to be an *authentic man*. I share this with you to get you excited about what the future holds for you, not only as a man, but as the Hero you will become.

1. Rejects Passivity. Makes decisions, acts based on doing the right thing, and has the courage to fight through feelings to follow through and do it. Man of Action!

2. Accepts Responsibility. Completely accepts responsibility for one's life, actions- past, present, and future. Also accepts responsibility for those you are entrusted with. No longer a victim of circumstance, but rather a victor over it.

3. Leads Courageously. Steps up to lead courageously, regardless of how hard it may be. Shows others the way when it's easier to just focus on self.

4. Expects the Greater Reward. Expects the greater reward for doing these things. The blessings that are received from the actions taken.

As you start to go through this Heroes Blueprint, you will start seeing these traits coming out in you. Others will start seeing these traits come out in you, too. And you will never be the same again.

Because here's the deal…

You were not meant to be a doctor, you were not meant to be a teacher, you were not meant to be a factory worker, you were not meant to be a pilot, you were not meant to be a politician, you were not meant to be an entrepreneur, and you were not meant to be a piano teacher. You were meant to be a Transformational Hero; everything else is just what you do. The sooner you figure this out in life, the sooner you will start to live.

THE HEART OF A HERO

"The greatness of a man's power is in the measure of his surrender."
William Booth, founder of the Salvation Army

I didn't want to write this chapter. I thought I was done with this book, and to be honest, I wanted to be finished. But what I wanted didn't matter, because there was something way bigger than me telling me to write on. It was not done.

Everything you've read up to this point has been straight from the heart and relentlessly real. I feel the bond that's been created between you and me through this process intensely, and I honestly hope to meet you some day, and hear your story.

This chapter is a great example of the inner battle that's faced when we're deciding whether to do what feels right (feelings), versus overcoming fear (courage) to do what we know is right. And the fact is, I have to share this with you in order to be 100% authentic, and to continue to have your trust in me.

You see, The Heroes Blueprint, and the implementation of these steps, has absolutely changed my life and the lives of others. There is no doubt about that, and there is no doubt that it will do the same for you. In a lot of cases, it will give you life in ways you didn't know existed. If I could offer a "Life Back Guarantee," I would, because there would be ZERO returns. I would be risking nothing to do that.

But the truth is, I've been trying most of my life to implement these steps, or something similar, in order to truly live out a life that was worthy of living. Maybe you feel the same way, to some extent. I mean, there probably really isn't anything within these pages that you haven't at least heard of before or thought of before yourself. The fact is, the framework, or step-by-step process, that lays out the Heroes Blueprint is what makes it something of real life-changing value. But going through this process will only leave you longing for more, if you aren't truly ready to do it.

I'm going to tell you a little story that I feel led to share. I'm hoping it will shed some light on this whole Heroes Blueprint and how to truly be ready for it. It's called "The Road to Kalispell."

The Road to Kalispell

I'm a Harley rider. I would have said motorcycle rider, but we all know that the only people who say they ride motorcycles are the ones who didn't buy a Harley. I know, I know, it's completely stupid and vain, but at least I am honest. The truth is, my Harley breaks down all the time, but as us Harley guys like to joke, we'd rather break down on a Harley than get there on anything else. Actually, some of the most fun on trips come from the unexpected break-downs in the middle of nowhere, USA with your buddies. Wives aren't so much excited about the thrill of the break-down as us guys. Anyway, if you ride motorcycles, please don't be offended; it's all in good fun. I would ride with you any day.

There really is something about getting on that steel horse, hearing the rumble of the exhaust, feeling the sun on your skin and tasting the road grime in your mouth. It's awesome. And that isn't even taking into account the new tough guy outfits you get to wear. Some Harley executive was once quoted as saying:

"What we sell is the ability for a 43-year-old accountant to dress in black leather, ride through small towns, and have people be afraid of him." *unknown Harley executive.*

Well, I'm not out to have people be afraid of me, but it's certainly fun to pretend like you're tough, at least for a weekend here and there.

I've been lucky enough to travel all over this country on my two-wheeled tough guy machine, and have been through 30 states as of now, I think; most of those states twice, and some three times. I would love to write a book about the travels I've had and the people I've met. It's been amazing. But there's one ride that I did alone that is the one I want to tell you about. Kalispell.

Ever heard of Kalispell? Me neither, until one morning, back in 2006, when I woke up with it on my mind. I had no idea what it was or meant or anything, so I went to Google it and found out. It turns out that Kalispell is a town in northwest Montana. Interesting, I guess, but I didn't give it much thought after that. Then I started having these weird Kalispell moments happen to me. One morning, I woke up with the name of this town I had never heard of before, and then all the sudden I am hearing about it all the time.

For the next three months, I kept having these moments. One moment would be from a co-worker who was talking about his aunt, who just happened to live in Kalispell, Montana. Weird, considering that I knew this guy for years and it never came up. Then another with a customer of mine, who, in a conversation about some of the pretty parts of the country, said out of the blue how beautiful this town was that he used to drive his truck through up in northwest Montana: Kalispell. Another when I was talking to a guy at a party who I'd never met before, and asked, "Where are you from, originally?"

He said, "Kalispell."

There was also a constant, nagging thought in my head about this town. A little like a whisper, but more like a yell. I remember thinking I must be crazy when I said out loud, "God, do you want me to go to Kalispell?" I remember thinking I heard, "Duh." I took that as a yes. Any logical person would just jump on their Harley and head that way. I didn't really think it was logical, so I kept it a secret. I was a little embarrassed to tell anybody. I mean what would I say when they asked, "Hey, Tim, why you going to Kalispell?" It's not like I could actually say, "Well, I think God is telling me to." (Enter cricket sound and deer in the headlights look.)

God had certainly been a big part of my life up until that point. I was dragged to church every since I was able to remember. I knew how to pray, in theory; I knew the basic Bible Scriptures and stories; I wasn't afraid to set foot in church; I had played in the church band, led worship at certain times, and from the outside looking in, depending on your viewpoint, I was a pretty standard Christian. Go to church, read some Bible stuff, maybe serve a little, do some good stuff, and pretty much continue to do whatever I wanted, regardless. God and I, at that point, had more of a relationship that mimicked the criminal and the bail bondsman. I would be the criminal in this deal, in case you were wondering.

I would do some Christian stuff, and then do whatever I wanted until that caught up with me and I needed him to bail me out again. Except that this was an emotional bailout. I would have said to anybody, at this point in my life, that I had really given my life to Christ and lived for him. The truth is, I believed it; I just didn't know how wrong I was. I was a break-even Christian. A little bit of God, a little bit of me, and hopefully I broke even.

So I packed up my Harley on a Wednesday and decided to head to Kalispell, Montana. I was about to find out why, or at least I was hoping to.

I remember leaving about 8 o'clock in the morning, thinking I would get to Sturgis, which is a town of nothing unless the big motorcycle rally was in town. I had a friend who had a townhome there, where I could stay for the night. It would be a long day, about 12 hours. As I hit the interstate I was thinking how crazy I was, and God had better have something good waiting for me in Kalispell, because I was taking off work to do this ridiculous trip. As I turned north on I-29, just outside of Omaha my bike started to act a little funny. It was running extremely rough, and I knew there was a problem. One of the cool things about riding so many miles on the same motorcycle is that you really start to feel as if it is an extension of yourself, and you begin to understand each and every vibration. They all tell you something, and this one was telling me to pull over. I found a little gas station and rolled in. Secretly, inside my mind, I was thinking that this was my chance to turn back, because I certainly could not continue on, worrying about my bike and whether it would get me there or not. I could have someone from Des Moines pick me up in two hours and be back home with the victory of knowing that at least I tried, and it's not my fault the bike broke down.

The mechanic working under the hood of an old Ford pickup heard me roll up and headed over. He looked like the type of guy who could put grease between two pieces of bread, call it a sandwich, and love it. My tough guy gear was not fooling him in the least. He asked me what was wrong and I just said it started to run rough, and I'm not sure what's wrong with it yet. He took one look and said, "It looks like to me you may have a lose wire there running over to your distributor thingy." That may not be exactly what he said, but it's what I heard. And sure enough, he was right. About two seconds after I pulled in, it was running better than ever. I asked how much I owed him, and he just said, "Forget about it, I wouldn't want to keep you from your ride. So you better get on with it."

I guess so, I thought.

Well, the rest of that day seemed pretty normal, at least for a 12-hour motorcycle ride. A lot of heat, some discomfort, sore butt, sunburned face, and great gas station sandwiches. I made it to Sturgis, got some food, spent the night, and woke up ready to head out the next morning. I left behind a note to thank my hosts for the stay, and a little oil in the driveway to remind them I was there.

I wasn't sure how far I'd get on the second day. I was still about 750 miles away from Kalispell, which is not impossible, but extremely painful, especially on my not-built-for-long-rides Harley. Little did I know that I would actually make it far enough to get my answer for why I was going.

It was about mile 600 that day, when I was coming around this curve and noticed the charcoal-colored clouds peeking over the mountain top. The rain was coming, and I was torqued. As far as I was concerned, if I was going to be following through with what I thought God was telling me to do, which was somewhat ridiculous anyway, at least he could give me good weather, if not perfect weather. In this part of Montana there may or may not be an exit for 50 miles. It was a real emotional low point when it started to rain. I was not wearing rain gear, because that really isn't my deal. I've ridden in sleet, snow, hail, rain, and everything outside of a tornado and would much rather pull off than ride through it. Usually pulling off isn't an issue, but in Montana, well, you never know. I vividly remember saying out loud as I looked up in the sky, "God, I really can't handle this freaking rain right now." Settled into my misery, I came around a corner of this small mountain and saw the most glorious sight I think I had seen up to that point in my life, and that was a little abandoned gas station with a canopy just big enough to fit under and keep me dry. I veered off the highway, made a beeline for this dry spot, and took a deep breath as my motorcycle came to a stop. I would wait out the rain. And God would start talking.

You see, up until that point in my life I was the break-even Christian. What I realized later on is what that really means is you're never really "All In" with anything. I wasn't all in with what the world had to offer, and I certainly wasn't all in with God, either. I was exactly what Scripture says in James 1:6, *"But when you ask, you must believe and not doubt, because the one who doubts is like a wave of the sea, blown and tossed by the wind."* I had no direction, and the feeling of turmoil I constantly carried inside me reflected how I felt like that wave being tossed around in this sea we call the world. I spent most of my prayer life asking God for direction because I felt so lost with jobs, relationships, family, money, etc., and then I would end up doing whatever I wanted. A very self-defeating pattern.

Well, I guess God had decided he was tired of hearing my empty prayers, and he wanted to really say something to me. He knew it would take me getting to that little abandoned gas station on the side of the road in the middle of Montana to get me to listen.

As I sat there on my bike, I started to go through the post-getting-poured-on-while-riding-your-Harley-process. Clean the fog off the goggles, ring out the bandana, and check the luggage to make sure no zippers are open. As I was going through this process I suddenly had an overwhelming feeling that explained everything. God spoke to me very clearly as I sat there that day on my Harley, wet and tired.

He said, *"Why would I waste my time giving you directions when you have never proven you would go?"*

Whoa... I thought. He was right. My whole life, I had been praying for this direction, but never proven that I would actually follow through with what I felt God was saying to me if it didn't fit my plans. He continued, *"And just when I knew you couldn't handle the rain I gave you shelter. You can pretty much count on this for everything else, as well, but first you have to go."*

I was dumbfounded. I felt very small and very excited at the same time. I knew everything he was saying to me was right on, and I felt it, deep within. After digesting this for a minute, I realized a couple of things.

The trip had nothing to do with Kalispell. It had everything to do with a test, by finding a spot that was far enough away to make me not want to go, but close enough to know I could probably make it.

God will always provide the tools, people, places, and things to accomplish his goals through us, if we just commit and go. He won't ever give us more than we can handle.

So, of course, the very next thought that came to me was, *Do I still have to go to Kalispell, now that I know the reason for the trip?*

I decided I didn't want to chance it, and I went. I spent that night in Missoula and then headed north, to Kalispell early the next morning. The trip was beautiful, and it is one of the most gorgeous areas that I've ever seen. When I got to Kalispell, about lunch time, I pulled into the Hardees there, had myself a hamburger, and headed out of town back to Des Moines, which would take me a couple of days. I had to make sure, you know, that there wasn't another surprise in Kalispell. I was "All In," for sure.

I'm assuming something about you, if you're still with me to this point in the book. I'm assuming that you either consider yourself someone of faith, or you are being drawn to find out what the tugging on your heart is that keeps you reading. Which is it?

You see, Kalispell taught me how to *listen, go, and trust*. And when God whispered to me to write this last chapter, I listened. I didn't want to, but I did, and now I'm going to trust that God is putting the right words on this piece of paper.

The Heroes Blueprint is something that will change your life, but the truth is that there are lots of things that will change your life. The self-help industry, which spits out "life changing" material every day, is a multi-billion dollar business every year, based on the fact that they say they can change your life.

There is no shortage of "life-changing" things in this world, but there is only one thing that can change our hearts, and that one thing is God. He cries out for our hearts more than anything in Isaiah 29:13, when he says, *"These people come near to me with their mouth and honor me with their lips, but their hearts are far from me. Their worship of me is based on merely human rules they have been taught."*

The truth is, I surrendered my life to God lots of times, probably thousands, if someone was keeping track. I continued to do it in order to break even on the life I was living. But I didn't feel like I was truly getting anywhere. And then one day I read Isaiah 29:13, and decided maybe God was saying something different than just surrender your life to me. Maybe he wanted my heart instead? So I started praying from that point on,

"God I surrender my heart completely to you. Take it and make it yours."

And, you see, that's when everything in my life started to change. That's when I started to go down this Heroes Blueprint that you find in your hands. I was no longer breaking even. The old destructive habits seemed to just fade away. That's when my relationships started to overflow in abundance in every way, and that's when I started to become effective and make a difference in this world that I could actually feel. It was tangible. I started getting traction.

A.W. Tozier said, "The reason why many are still troubled, still seeking, still making little forward progress, is because they haven't yet come to the end of themselves. We're still trying to give orders, and interfering with God's work within us."

It wasn't until I invited God in to change my heart that my life changed. It was that easy. I guess you could say that was the moment I finally came to the end of myself.

You can go through the Heroes Blueprint and let it change your life, no doubt about it. Or better yet, you can surrender your heart to God and let your life follow with changes you can't possibly imagine.

If you do that, implementing the Heroes Blueprint in your life will be as natural as breathing, and you can absolutely change the world by becoming a Hero who transforms your life and the lives of those around you.

NEXT STEPS

So now what?

Well first off, I want you to know that implementing these 10 steps isn't something that you should feel stressed out about. It takes a little time and that's really by design. If it was super quick and easy, then we probably would miss the character development that comes from perseverance, patience, and time.

What I would do very first thing is to re-read the book and use a pen to mark up the pages, take notes, write down ideas that come to your mind and basically absorb the information.

Then the second thing I would do is to just start going through each step. Whether it takes a week or a month for each one really doesn't matter. What I want is for you to feel like you either have a concrete understanding of each concept, or that you have finished the exercise if there is one, and you feel ready to move on to the next step. As you start checking off the steps, you will gain the momentum that will propel you into having this Heroes Blueprint implemented in your life. When that happens it will become part of who you are, and you will not have to think about it anymore. You will simply take each step and by nature start to go deeper into your understanding of how you can be more effective within each area.

So go back through The Heroes Blueprint and start to check off the steps as you implement them into your life.

RESOURCES TO CONSIDER

Courses to Start the Gutting Process:

- The Quest For Authentic Manhood
  Website http://www.mensfraternity.com

- Christ Life Course- Website http://www.christlifesolution.com

URL to print out the 49 Qualities Of Christ exercise:

- http://www.timmitchum.com/thb/49qualities

Mentoring Resources:

- The Book "As Iron Sharpens Iron" Howard Hendricks and William Hendricks

- The Book "The Mentor Leader" Tony Dungy

- Big Brothers Big Sisters http://www.bbbs.org

- YMCA http://www.ymca.net/

- A list of different Mentoring opportunities by state can be found on this website as well http://www.mentoring.org/about_mentor/mentoring_partnerships

- Fellowship Of Christian Athletes (FCA) http://www.fca.org

Other Books/Resources/Courses to look into:

- The Book "The Purpose Driven Life" by Rick Warren
- The Book "The Secret Life Of The Soul" by J. Keith Miller
- Financial Peace University
  http://www.daveramsey.com/fpu/home/
- The Book "Winners Never Cheat" by Jon M. Huntsman

ACKNOWLEDGEMENTS

I consider myself extremely lucky to have always had a sense of faith in my life of something bigger than myself. It has been a constant struggle to figure out who to live for, God or myself, for most of my life. I am most thankful that He has continued to show up to battle for my soul every day. Because of His relentless persistence I finally solidified who I would be living for, and now just have to figure out how I can do it better every day so that I end up the Hero I was created to be. So thank you for fighting for me when I really probably wasn't that much of a prize.

To my mom, Michelle, Jeff, Doug, Katie, Cera, Nessee, Willow and H. You continued to put up with me for a lot of years and I thank you for that. I used to be the one who always had to "get going" and now it seems you have to kick me out. Funny how things changed when I implemented this blueprint.

To Hop, without your unconditional love, belief and support in me I highly doubt this project would have gotten done. Every day you teach me more about how to truly love someone.

To Robert Deitch, Ed Nichols, Troy Salazar, and Dr. Bob Stouffer, I can't tell you how much your time through mentoring, reviewing and giving me feedback means. Not only was the value you added immeasureable but the time spent together was priceless to me.

To Kirt Eldredge, I thank you and love you for being the first man willing to show up for me. I always knew you were watching and that gave me a reason to finish whatever race in life I was in. Without you I wouldn't have such a strong handshake and be opening every door I can for anybody walking through one still to this day. I just wish we would have gotten to the tying a tie part. ;) I still read from a bible you gave to me years ago. I thank you for giving me an example of a man worth following.

To the group of close friends that I am blessed with having in my life, Ryan Roe, Johnny Moller, Dennis Bailey, Jason Stecker, Jessica Vandenburg, Ryan Kinart, Tony Burroughs, Duane Tolander, Nathan Manning, Donny Vestal, and Lew Major. Thank you for allowing me to be a part of your life and your families' lives.

A special thanks to Jon Hunstman Sr., Robert Lewis, and Howard Hendrichs for letting me use stories from your books and programs to add value to mine.

It's impossible to thank everyone who has helped in getting this message out, and if I have forgotten anyone please accept my sincere apology. I really do appreciate you.

Finally I want to thank YOU for taking the time to let me share my story with you and hopefully give you some insight on how you can live and end your life as the Hero you were meant to be.

ABOUT THE AUTHOR

Tim Mitchum is a successful online entrepreneur and sales professional. He is also the author of multiple books including the *Common Sense Conversations For Couples Series* and *The Heroes Blueprint*. He completely turned his life around through implementing the 10 steps in *The Heroes Blueprint* and now enjoys spending his time devoted to seeing that others have the same opportunity, through leading small groups, mentoring, speaking, coaching, and online programs. He resides in Des Moines, Iowa, and when he isn't spending time with family and friends, he is riding his Harley through the small towns of Iowa pretending to be a tough guy. You can meet Tim and get some really cool free stuff by going to www.TimMitchum.com.

CPSIA information can be obtained at www.ICGtesting.com
Printed in the USA
LVOW011522120112

263543LV00001B/3/P